BITCOIN AND CRYPTOCURRENCY TRADING FOR BEGINNERS

MUST HAVE GUIDE TO START ACHIEVING YOUR FINANCIAL FREEDOM TODAY. TOOLS, WALLETS, ANALYSIS, CHARTS, BEST EXCHANGES, TIPS AND STRATEGIES, DISCIPLINE.

MARK WARREN ANDERSON

Table of Contents

Introduction

What Is Cryptocurrency

Cryptocurrency is a digital or virtual currency exchanged for goods and services, just like the more common fiat money. But there are some key differences. Cryptocurrencies use cryptography to secure and verify transactions on a distributed public ledger using open-source code. This means that anyone holding the cryptocurrency has access to it in its original form.

History

The first cryptocurrency was bitcoin, established in 2009 by an anonymous programmer as an open-source code project on GitHub. Today there are many other cryptocurrencies such as Ethereum, Litecoin, Dash, etc., with varying degrees of popularity and complexity in design; they are often collectively referred to as altcoins.

The concept of cryptocurrency emerged at the beginning of 2009 when an anonymous creator known as Satoshi Nakamoto published a Bitcoin paper: A Peer-to-Peer Electronic Cash System project website, GitHub. The idea was to create a currency independent from any central authority, transferable electronically, more or less instantly, with meager transaction fees.

By the end of 2010, bitcoin was trading at less than $0.01 per coin on an online exchange market. By the end of 2011, bitcoin reached $1 per coin. In November 2013, it crossed the $1000 threshold per coin, which gave rise to serious concerns regarding its safety in light of recent developments on Mt Gox exchange where thousands of bitcoins were stolen by hackers.

The value of 3,000 bitcoins that Mt Gox lost is now valued at $30 million. In the third week of 2013, another essential bitcoin exchange called Bitstamp suspended operations due to what appeared to be a technical issue. Later investigations by investigative journalists revealed that Bitstamp had suffered a security breach and hackers had stolen more than $5 million worth of bitcoins from their hot wallets.

In the fourth quarter of 2013, another major bitcoin exchange called Mt Gox filed for bankruptcy when it suspended its service, citing a DDoS (Distributed Denial of Service) attack on its computer systems triggered by unknown hackers. This led to over $473 million worth of bitcoins being lost and sent ripples throughout the bitcoin community.

To this day, bitcoin has experienced several significant price fluctuations, rising from less than $0.01 to $20,000. In 2013 it was the fastest-growing currency in the world. It is well on its way to becoming a global payment method for many businesses and individuals in the 21st century.

How Cryptocurrency Works

Bitcoin's initial function was a cryptocurrency, but it has evolved into something much more significant (see What Bitcoin is?). It is not just a currency for payments or online purchases but also serves as an electronic platform for storing wealth like gold and silver in conventional banking systems with little or no risk of theft due to digitalization and encryption technologies used by bitcoin.

Cryptocurrencies are designed to be completely decentralized, with a limited number of nodes or servers that can process transactions. They are "mined" by solving a set of complex algorithms, usually using hardware as powerful as graphics cards or processors and then stored in an encrypted digital wallet. Blockchain technology (see What Blockchain Technology is?) used in the cryptocurrency system enables users to access their digital currency from any location in the world without maintaining a physical wallet.

The blockchain is a public ledger where all cryptocurrency transactions are stored. The wallet owner can access it via their private key, which acts as an identifier and password. The private key is used to sign transactions and authorize withdrawals from the account, verified by network nodes.

The transaction details are then added to the blockchain by nodes that have verified the sender of the payment and were accepted by majority consensus. The cryptocurrency then moves between wallets. As time goes on and more people use a cryptocurrency, its value grows by demand and supply factors. This is similar to how gold and silver rose in value when demand rises and supply falls.

Advantages and Disadvantages

As the world becomes increasingly digital, many are turning to virtual currencies. There are many advantages to using cryptocurrency: no exchange rate hassles, you can carry a wallet on your phone so that you can spend money anywhere, and it also presents more security. However, there are disadvantages as well: some retailers refuse to take cryptocurrencies for transactions; also, some governments have instituted heavy regulations on them for use in the country of origin.

Types

Other cryptocurrencies have been developed over time based on bitcoin's underlying technology (see What Blockchain Technology is?). They include Litecoin, Ethereum, and Ripple. Each of these coins is competing with bitcoin to become the most popular cryptocurrency worldwide.

Introduction to Bitcoin

Bitcoin is a form of digital money or currency held in cyberdeposits without any physical embodiment like banknotes or coins. It is difficult to counterfeit and can be sent electronically from one person to another without the need for a central authority or any middle man. It is not controlled by a central bank like gold, government bonds, or other forms of money. Nor is it backed by any government or bank.

History of Bitcoins

It was established in 2009 by an anonymous programmer as an anonymous open-source project on GitHub with the alias Satoshi Nakamoto. The original project name was Bitcoin: A Peer-to-Peer Electronic Cash System. Still, this name has been abandoned as per the recommendations of a working group that includes core developers and Bitcoin Foundation representatives, suggesting that the bitcoin protocol should no longer be considered a peer-to-peer system.

The primary cryptocurrency has emerged as a new asset class in international finance with a market capitalization of over $200 million when writing this book. Bitcoin's price has experienced a meteoric rise from less than $0.01 in 2010 to over $20,000 by mid-2018

Why Trade Bitcoins

Bitcoin benefits its users by offering them a wide range of applications such as peer-to-peer payments, source of funds, investment assets, and a hedge against traditional market volatility. By design, bitcoin's blockchain technology cannot be controlled by any single authority. Its independence from central regulators also means that it is not subject to government regulations such as taxation, but this also makes it vulnerable to theft and fraud without regulation or protection by the authorities. This has made bitcoin somewhat volatile, with wild price swings representing a significant risk for investors or traders of cryptocurrencies.

Bitcoin is a digital currency at its most superficial level, but it can also be seen as the first global currency for the internet age. It offers excellent value for money, easy transferability, and various applications. It can be used to pay for purchases online, as an investment asset class, and hedge against traditional market volatility by converting it to fiat currencies like the US dollar or British pound.

About Other Cryptocurrencies

The Bitcoin protocol handles two functions: first, verify and record transactions made with bitcoins, and second, to create new bitcoins in each transaction. New bitcoins get created when network nodes compete to solve complex computer algorithms for which the winner gets rewarded with bitcoins. The reward gets divided among all the nodes that participated in the verification process.

Bitcoin is a decentralized currency, and network nodes verify its transactions without any central verification. It is a peer-to-peer network that operates without any single point of failure. All it requires is an internet connection, which could be either cellular or Wi-Fi.

The system was designed to operate in two ways: as a cryptocurrency and as a wallet for storing wealth with the expectation that its value would increase over time. Cryptocurrencies like bitcoin are designed to be used as an electronic payment system, not just as an investment asset class.

Learning the Lingo

Bitcoin has been around for ten years, but not many people know the bitcoin lingo.

What Is a Bitcoin Wallet?

A bitcoin wallet is where you store your bitcoins once you have exchanged them for Norwegian kroner or another currency. There are several types of wallets, each with different levels of security and functionality:

- Online web-based wallets (third parties host these).

- Mobile apps (these are downloadable apps that provide access to the private keys).

- Hardware wallets (these are small devices that plug into your computer's USB port and enable you to spend bitcoins without internet access).

- Paper wallets (these are pieces of paper with the address and private key printed on them).

Is it safe?

All wallet types listed above can be stored online or offline. When you store bitcoins offline, in a hardware or paper wallet, they are "cold"—not connected to the internet. You can also store bitcoins offline in a mobile app, but the app would have to be downloaded from an online app provider and configured offline using an air gap to protect your privacy.

Where Can I Get a Bitcoin Wallet?

You can get a bitcoin wallet from an online service provider, such as Coinbase. Or, you can download the original Bitcoin client (available for free on Bitcoin.org) and create a wallet on your computer.

Each wallet provider will give you a public Bitcoin address—this is the address others will use to send Bitcoins to you. If someone sends Bitcoins to your address, they are stored in your account until you are ready to spend them or exchange them for another currency.

Suppose you choose an online service provider (like Coinbase). In that case, it is a good idea to immediately move your coins into a mobile or hardware wallet that only you control after receiving them.

How Do I Get Bitcoins?

There are three basic ways to obtain bitcoins:

- Buy them through an online service provider.
- Mine them using your own computer's processing power.
- Exchange them for cash or another cryptocurrency, such as Ethereum.

Bitcoin mining is the process of using your computer's processing power to help facilitate and verify transactions on the blockchain—a shared public ledger of transactions that everyone can access but no single person controls or owns. You are rewarded with bitcoins only if you provide this service (called "hashing") efficiently, and on time, so it makes sense to join a mining pool for greater efficiency.

What Are Bitcoin Mining Pools?

A mining pool is a group of miners who combine resources such as processing power, advanced hardware, and computers with the most effective bitcoin mining software installed. You can participate by joining a mining pool with others. If you share your resources, you will earn proportionally more bitcoins per block solved.

Who Are the Most Significant Bitcoin Miners?

Bitcoins have not been mined in large quantities yet; the largest miner is:

Bitcoin miner Antpool—If Antpool breaks the current BTC/USD rate daily, it was enough to justify itself as one of the world's biggest Bitcoin mines for as long as it takes to settle this business.

Chapter 1. Comprehending Cryptocurrency Market Cycles

Let's imagine we bought some coins that we don't know anything about based on simple technical analysis for $10, and we find ourselves 24 hours later with the same coins, which dropped to $8. How would we manage the loss? What would happen is that the doubt of having invested in a dying, useless project or on the usual inevitable package would become an exhausting worm that would push us to sell; perhaps in the middle of a dump, perhaps at the lowest possible price (with the greatest possible damage.) It happens more frequently than you might imagine.

On the other hand, if we had bought some coins that we know well, having analyzed in detail the project on which we invested our money, then enduring a collapse from $10 to $8 becomes more accessible. However good a trader can be in technical analysis, it becomes challenging to trade cryptocurrencies without fundamental analysis. We have already had the opportunity to explain that fundamental analysis can be understood as collecting information by reading the company's financial statements in the stock market. Still, it is a pity that when we talk about cryptocurrencies most of the time, there is no company at all, let alone a budget.

However, there are factors that we can take into consideration, such as market capitalization (market cap.) By capitalizing on a cryptocurrency, we mean the total amount we obtain by multiplying the number of coins in circulation by the value of those coins. Another evaluation that we must make in this sense is to distinguish the maximum supply (21 million coins, for example, if we are talking about BTC) from that available (circulating.) Today, there are about 17,5 million BTC in circulation, compared to a maximum number of coins that will ever end up on the market equal to 21 million.

The quantity of coins in circulation, with the maximum number of coins that the network has budgeted, is one factor to study for a new cryptocurrency. For an accurate fundamental analysis, we should be able to disassemble the code of the open-source platform and understand how it is made, how it works, and above all, if it is well done. Not many people have the skills to do an accurate fundamental analysis of a blockchain project, who knows how to "disassemble" the platform and understand how it works. Ordinary people, who do not have excellent computer skills, therefore have other ways to try to understand if we can trust or not.

The very first things that every cryptocurrency trader wants to know when investing his money are about the community (the nodes and users in the network) and the identity of the people involved in developing the project. When we are faced with a coin that thousands of people spend every day and processed by its blockchain through a sufficiently large and decentralized network of nodes, we are already moderately sure that we are dealing with the sound starting material.

But there are other details that we are interested in knowing, especially with developers who carry out the project. Each cryptocurrency should have its official website, and within the official website, there must necessarily be a part in which the leading figures within the community are mentioned. If there is a company or nonprofit behind a project, then figures such as the CEO, department heads, and other executives should also be indicated.

If, on the other hand, there is neither a company nor a foundation behind a project, then on the website, there should be a shred of the "about us" part in which the developers are mentioned. What we need to understand is who are the people most exposed in the project: if they are serious people, if they are established, esteemed, or not. In short, the more we know, the better.

Even a project led by a good, brilliant, and capable person can end up shipwrecked, and even "famous" people can throw a package at you. But in general, the quality of any project is always closely linked to the quality of the people who take care of it. Suppose we have a decentralized network worthy of the name, with thousands of users who spend that cryptocurrency every day, a team of developers known and respected internationally. In that case, we have a whole series of signals that are very useful for building that indispensable trust.

However, all this is not enough. It is necessary to know the project more in-depth, understand how it works and what opportunities it can offer. To do this, you start by reading a document ("white paper") that all the teams disseminate and update periodically. All the characteristics and peculiarities of the project should be reported, and it should describe in detail how the technology works.

The white papers should be understood more as advertising brochures than as information documents (after all, no one would ever put pen to paper that their project is useless, does not work, or has no future.) From reading them, we can still obtain helpful information; if a particular currency, for example, uses a consensus protocol that I already know and do not trust, then it will make little sense to invest in that cryptocurrency.

Suppose I find that the ambition of this new coin that I want to invest in is simply to be yet another blockchain-based payment system. In that case, I will probably think that there are older and more reliable coins to keep an eye on and that I am not interested in investing my money on what appears to be only the millionth copy of true innovation.

Suppose again I discover that the platform on which I want to invest, which on paper offers dozens of exciting services (from the creation of new tokens to the management of the intelligent contract,) is still far behind the other platforms preside over the same segment of the market. In that case, I will probably be inclined to want to wait a little longer before investing. Based on all this information we collect and the different evaluations that each time directly derive from each different information collected, we develop our conviction about a particular project, we define which coins we trust most and which least, with which we feel comfortable operating and which ones we prefer not to deal with.

Of the eight hundred and more cryptocurrencies available on the market (without counting the tokens), it will be enough to isolate twenty of those we like best and concentrate on looking for our trading signals for only those twenty; even so, we must understand that fundamental analysis is something that must be carried out daily, and includes all the information and news gathering activity that we have to do practically every day.

Since news moves the market, arriving first on the news means taking advantage over other traders; to do this, there are a series of profitable operations to do, such as follow the developer accounts on social networks, subscribe to the official newsletters, the telegram channel, participate in discussions on the forums where the community meets. In short, any channel that can provide us with news in advance of other traders must be opened and probed frequently.

Once we have defined a group of cryptocurrencies that we trust, studied their charts, collected information on the technology and the people leading the project, and are ready to intercept any new news and having our trading strategy made up of precise rules, then we will have all the tools that allow us to trade cryptocurrencies profitably.

Chapter 2. Best Platforms

Cryptocurrencies 2.0, also known as "platform" cryptocurrencies, were born from the idea of Vitalik Buterin, who is a Canadian programmer of Russian descent. He is the inventor of Ethereum, designed in 2013 when he was just 20 years old. The idea of the Canadian programmer was to exploit the 360-degree blockchain technology, not limiting its use to the application in the world of cryptocurrencies. Almost parallel to Buterin's idea, another similar operating platform developed, that of NEO.

The platforms are a development of web 3.0 because they aim to allow the widespread diffusion of the "Smart Economic" through the large-scale development of applications, shared software, and smart contracts. The opensource structure favors the development of the Smart Economy in these platforms, and in general, by the possibility of sharing information among all users. Each application and software can be downloaded for free by users, and their scripts are "open" to any person who wants to consult them.

Ethereum

Ethereum, unlike Bitcoin, is not just a cryptocurrency; it is a decentralized platform for managing intelligent contracts. While Bitcoin is intended to serve as a virtual medium of exchange, Ethereum founder Vitalik Burerim did not want to limit his project to just this function. The concept of a platform is much broader than that of cryptocurrency. The Ethereum platform is also a cryptocurrency. The coin that runs in the Ethereum network is precisely the Ether (ETH in the acronym). Still, its main feature is being a platform within which it is possible to develop applications, software, and "Smart Contract." The operation of these contracts is embodied in the programming of applications that autonomously perform exactly what was programmed at the time of the agreement between the parties. This way, there is no possibility of downtime, censorship, fraud, or interference from third parties. Buterin's idea, when he started developing Ethereum in 2013, was to make the most of the blockchain's potential. He believed that using technology as a simple "ledger" for exchanging a cryptocurrency was limiting.

The development of Ethereum began in 2013, and the first version of the software became available starting in February 2014. Since then, many software versions have been made public that have introduced and developed three new programming languages for writing Smart Contracts.

To finance the platform's development, Ether was launched for the first time in a public pre-sale offer, in a form similar to that of IPOs (initial public offerings), which made it possible to raise about $19 million in BTC.

In extreme simplicity, Ethereum could be presented as the most significant shared computer that is capable of delivering enormous power available everywhere and forever. In other words, Ethereum is a computational platform that is "remunerated" through exchanges that are carried out through Ether. It is a platform that can be adopted by all those who wish to become part of the network and who, in this way, will have a solution that allows all participants to have a shared and immutable archive. The Ethereum project is flexible and suitable for use in different application areas; it can be defined as a "Programmable Blockchain" that not only allows you to carry out predefined and standardized "operations" but allows users to create their own "operations."

The basis of the functioning of the entire Ethereum network is the platform's cryptocurrency, Ether. It is used for carrying out all transactions and operations within the platform. For example, a user who wants to "run" his contract within Ethereum must pay for this service to the system in Ether. Similarly, a developer of an application or software through the platform must "pay" for the service offered by Ethereum. The payment may have either payments of Ether held by the subject or through the subject's "work," granting one's computational power to guarantee the Ethereum system.

Regarding the functioning of the Ethereum blockchain, it has the same characteristics as the Bitcoin one: a fundamental function is that performed by the "miners" who create the blocks and validate the transactions. A block is generated every 15 seconds on average, and as a reward for their work, miners receive 15 Ether per block. The system has not foreseen a maximum number of Ether that can be emitted; for this reason, there is currently around 100 million Ether in circulation. According to what is currently foreseen by the system, the number of Ether will continue to increase constantly, according to the predetermined pattern. However, it cannot be ruled out that programmers may propose a change to the unlimited growth of Ether which, if accepted by the network, could lead to a gradual reduction of their emission, such as the example with Bitcoin.

Smart Contract

The distinctive feature of Ethereum and its most important innovation is the introduction of "Smart Contracts." Smart contracts are computer protocols that facilitate, verify, or enforce, negotiate partial or total execution of a contract. In short, they are contracts that are executed automatically by a system. With contracts of this type, many contractual clauses can be made partially or fully automated, self-fulfilling, or both. Smart contracts aspire to ensure greater security than existing contracts and to reduce costs of the transaction associated with bargaining.

The Ethereum platform itself guarantees intelligent contracts responsible for authorizing, validating, and authenticating contracts.

NEO

NEO is the second most crucial blockchain platform after Ethereum; it is a Chinese developer project launched shortly after Ethereum in February 2014, aiming to compete with the first platform. NEO's ambitious goal is to help economic change through the development of the "Smart Economy." The NEO project manages intelligent contracts and software development on its platform utilizing payment with the platform's coin, the NEO. The platform works through a blockchain whose blocks are generated at intervals of 15 seconds each. The functioning of the network is always guaranteed by the miners, who create and authenticate in blocks and are therefore rewarded for their work with an amount of cryptocurrency.

While admitting the similarity of their project compared to the Ethereum one, the NEO programmers identify an advantage in scalability (i.e., the number of operations authenticated by their blockchain every second). An essential difference concerning Ethereum is that NEO supports various computer languages in everyday use, such as Microsoft and Java. On the other hand, Ethereum requires specific knowledge of its programming languages. Another difference between the NEO and the Ethereum project lies in the quantity of NEO units that can be issued, and the limit is set at 100 million units.

NEO units are not divisible; in fact, it is impossible to buy, for example, at 0.5 NEO. The number of NEOs that can be held must always be an integer. For this reason, for operations within the network, the "GAS" is used as an exchange cryptocurrency, a cryptocurrency subordinate to NEO, but operating in the same network. Anyone who holds NEOs for a certain period in their portfolio receives a quantity of GAS proportional to the amount of NEO held as if it were a kind of "dividend." In this way, NEO holders have an incentive to hold the cryptocurrency for a long time.

ICO

The ICO (Initial Coin Offering) is a fundraiser through which a "Token" or a "Coin" is offered through a blockchain platform in exchange for fiat currency or another cryptocurrency (such as Ether, NEO, or Bitcoin).

ICOs take place within platforms such as Ethereum and NEO and are implemented through a Smart Contract. Here, a Smart Contract is generated so that the two counterparties are: the company or the person who wants to place the Token or Coin on the market; the person who intends to sign the ICO. The subscriber will receive the cryptocurrency placed on the market at the deadline set by the contract through this contract. The proceeds raised through the ICO are used to finance the business or project of those who launched the offer.

The financing mechanism through the ICOs is reminiscent of that carried out by companies that want to go public through the IPO (Initial Public Offering). While similar in scope, the ICO is profoundly different from the initial public offering. Firstly, cryptocurrencies are digital assets, but they do not fall within a financial instrument regulated by lawmakers. The parties listed to participate in an IPO are protected by the law and have the right not to purchase the newly issued shares until the day the share is listed. The most important thing to point out is that when those who participate in an IPO buy the shares of a company, they become shareholders.

The token or coin object of the ICOs can be exchanged and used as a regular cryptocurrency. Their operation and the authentication of their transactions occur in the identical blockchain as the platform they launched.

Those who "launch" the ICO, referred to as "sponsors," usually provide access to a "white paper" describing the project, key team members, and key terms of the ICO (for example, the terms financial statements, contract details, and timing).

In the underwriting process, the participant is typically required to transfer cryptocurrency or a fiat currency to one or more designated addresses or the ICO "sponsor" online wallet. Registrations can be completed in minutes. An entity can also be rewarded with ICO tokens by doing some tasks for the issuing company, such as marketing on cryptocurrency forums. Once the ICO is complete, the ICO tokens are distributed to the participants' designated addresses or online wallets.

Chapter 3. Must-Have Tools

If you think of trading cryptocurrency, you should realize that crypto trading instruments can help you make the process easy. In this part, we will examine the best crypto trading tools accessible for novices that will support your possibilities of settling on better choices.

Coinmarketcap – for Coin/Token Information

Coinmarketcap is a crypto trading device that gives financial investors the constant fiat value of their traded cryptocurrency. Aside from this, the site gives essential data, for example, where your digital currency is listed, historical price, charts, and only the tip of the iceberg. This also lets you map out your investment strategy thoroughly.

Tradingview – for Technical Analysis

Tradingview offers a network of crypto financial investors, where novices can check the specialized analysis of their preferred digital money from specialists. Crypto trading consistently requires a thorough analysis of the coin market, and, ideally, you utilize this tool.

Bitcointalk – for Learning

This is an online Forum where crypto lovers worldwide meet to learn and share their insight on the crypto market. This is an ideal platform, to begin with for cryptocurrency beginners.

Reddit-r/Digital Currencies

Reddit is home to a large number of networks dependent on individuals' interests. The cryptocurrency community covers all themes about digital currencies and offers various perspectives concerning the market, exchanging regulation, and any tip of data you may discover fascinating.

Chapter 4. Must-Have Wallets

What we're talking about is a software application. The app could reside on your computer, phone, tablet, or another digital device. It could also reside somewhere on the internet. It could live on a removable hard drive, or even a thumb drive, enabling it to be cold stored safely away from other digital sources.

With this software, you can create your public wallet address or key. This is like a bank account number, your unique bitcoin identifier. You'll need it to receive, send and store your bitcoin. Your wallet also houses the private keys that are attached to your bitcoin. You need both to interact on the Bitcoin network.

The most common wallet types to date are:

Paper Wallet

Paper wallets are, as their name implies, a way to store both your private and public Bitcoin keys on paper. You create paper wallets via a paper wallet generator. These programs generate keys on your computer so that none of your private information exists on the internet. They allow you to "play around" with the keys, moving your mouse around to add to the randomization of the keys.

The keys are printed out, and they are usually also provided in QR format, allowing you to scan them to perform transactions.

This method of cold storage is a bit controversial. Some people consider it obsolete, as in a couple of years old. In their opinion, a paper wallet is about the most unsafe way you can "secure" your bitcoin because it involves printing out the information and storing it in paper form. Whenever you are using paper, it vastly increases the chances of someone else getting their grubby hands on your bitcoin. However, there are enough people who swear by paper wallets that it's worth considering. Paper wallets have the advantage of being impervious to hacking. The only way you can use the contents is to scan the QR code or manually enter the key into an online location. Paper wallets are quite popular, whether used temporarily or for the long term.

With paper wallets, their security rests squarely on your shoulders; your actions determine how "secure" are your bitcoin. And remember: if something happens to that piece of paper, say, it's damaged in flood or your dog eats it–your private keys are lost forever; you're out of luck with no way chance of ever reaccessing them. Without your keys, you can't get at your bitcoin, and it'll be unused forever, floating around the Bitcoin universe with no hope for reclamation.

You can minimize the risk of using paper wallets by adopting one or more of these practices:

Ensure that you are offline when you generate your wallet. Some people go so far as to download the application from another computer onto a thumb drive, install it on a computer that will never be connected to the internet, and generate keys that way. They also use a "dumb" printer, connected by cable to this computer, for printing.

Print off three copies, store one in a safe deposit box, another in a home safe, and the third with your attorney.

Use printable plastic; it won't age or deteriorate like paper.

Fold the paper in half, so the private key is hidden.

Affix a seal over the folded key; you can find seals that are "tamper-evident" so nobody can open them and replace the seal without you knowing it.

Refuse to store these keys on any electronic device, ever; otherwise, you're defeating the purpose of cold storage.

Use a form of password protection known as BIP-38. This adds another layer of security, making the paper keys worthless without it.

In addition to the cold storage option, paper bitcoin wallets make a unique and valuable gift, especially when you want to introduce a friend to the whole universe of cryptocurrency. A paper wallet is a delightful way to show your appreciation to a person who's helped you. Instead of a birthday gift card, you can give something unique: a paper Bitcoin wallet. A paper wallet can make a thoughtful wedding gift; in addition to the currency value, you are making it easier for the newlyweds to start their married life on a fresh financial footing.

Of course, your recipient will need their wallet to transfer and use any bitcoin you give them. They will need to be willing to get involved in Bitcoin, but I'm sure you'd be willing to help them along, using your own newly acquired cryptocurrency skills.

Hardware Wallet

Another way to store your bitcoin away from the prying eyes of internet hackers and nasty viruses is to use a hardware wallet. You stash your wallet on an external hard drive, a thumb drive, or another data storage device that can be unhooked from the internet.

This form of cold storage is very secure. You can now purchase cryptocurrency hardware wallets from $25 up to around $100. These dedicated wallets offer rock-solid security, offline private key generation, and virus protection. They're also designed to be easy to use, making them the ideal solution for the newcomer to Bitcoin. The most popular hardware wallets are currently TREZOR, KeepKey, and Ledger Nano S.

Mobile Wallet

Bitcoin wallets are not all that different from other software you've downloaded onto your phone; the same security measures apply. To spend bitcoin that is stored in your wallet, your private key is downloaded and installed on your phone. From a security point of view, you minimize the risk of your private key is picked up by others if it's isolated on your phone.

Mobile wallets are very convenient. Usually, you will have your phone with you, and that's all you'll need to access your Bitcoin wallet. A smartphone with internet access will let you perform bitcoin transactions as you move about.

The danger arises when your private key becomes vulnerable to unauthorized access. You'll want to back it up immediately after you have installed your chosen Bitcoin wallet. Regardless of which mobile wallet you choose, the software will contain a backup feature. You can also export a copy of your backup to cloud services or email it to yourself.

The most vital security measure is the authentication process. This is put in place to prevent funds from being misused or stolen off of your phone. Most mobile wallets come with an embedded PIN. The PIN must be entered before the user can access the wallet, just as you would with a debit card. When the wrong PIN is entered a certain number of times, the wallet will lock, and the instructions for how to unlock it will be sent via email or text to the owner. Or course, you'll want to set it up so a notification will be sent to an app not accessible by your phone!

Undoubtedly, when we talk about security and convenience, mobile wallets are your best bet, but the strength of your security depends entirely on you, the user. If you forget to back up your private key or if you leave your phone open for others to use, you are making yourself highly vulnerable to loss, whether by the permanent loss of the key or by the theft of an unsecured device and all its contents.

Bitcoin gives the user full responsibility and complete control every step of the way; this is why people like Bitcoin, after all. Yet, the flip-side of this freedom means you're entirely responsible for its security. While entirely up to you, protecting your cell phone wallet is essential enough that I would urge you to seriously consider the practical steps you can take to secure your wallets.

Web Wallet

Some companies offer wallet services for use with bitcoin. They serve as middlemen who will hold your coins and enable you to deposit and spend your bitcoin as you wish. Technically, the middleman takes away the hassle of security and administration for your account. However, this presents a single step away from the independent control that cryptocurrencies were established to bypass. Any wallet services company will require your personal information. Of course, this doesn't help at all if you are hoping to remain anonymous.

If you decide to go with a third-party wallet provider, make sure you trust the company. I say this because, already in Bitcoin's brief history, we have seen Bitcoin holding companies disappear, go bust, or be hacked, leaving customers in the lurch with no way to get back their precious bitcoin.

Generally, you need to proceed with caution as the regulation side of Bitcoin is still under development in some areas of the world. I recommend you select a country with solid regulations already in place that are friendly to cryptocurrencies. As of this writing, the Isle of Wight, the United Kingdom, and the United States are a few of the safest choices.

Software Wallet

Software wallets are designed to add to a computer's hard drive. This is a highly secure way to hold your bitcoin because the only way they can be accessed is from your computer. The software is fully supported, created, and developed by Bitcoin and is referred to as Bitcoin Core.

Public and Private Keys

Your Bitcoin wallet is more than an address; it also is where your private and public keys for your Bitcoin addresses are held. Your private key consists of a random mixture of numbers and letters related mathematically to your Bitcoin wallet address. This key cannot be hacked since a highly encrypted algorithm governs it.

You'll want to back up your private key frequently. Don't lose it; as I've already stated, there's no way to retrieve the information if it's destroyed. Thousands of bitcoin cannot be accessed already because the owners lost their keys or died without passing on the essential private information.

You also have a public key. This is the cause of considerable confusion because most people mistakenly think their Bitcoin wallet's address is the same as their public key. Your wallet address is your public key, a code that has been scrambled to provide some security. Your address is 160 bits in length.

You use your public key to confirm that you own the address and open it to send and receive funds. The public key is also based on a mathematical version of the private key. However, the relationship is so complicated that it would take millions of years for even the most powerful computer to crack it!

In addition to keys and the wallet address, your wallet also retains a log of all transactions, incoming and outgoing. Each transaction that is linked to your address is stored by your wallet so that you can see what you have spent and received at any given time. The wallet also stores the user preferences you have set up. The available preferences depend on the wallet type you are using and the platform you choose to serve as its host. Novice users will find life less complicated by using Bitcoin Core Client software. The preferences it offers are minimal, making it far easier to conquer the fundamental issues of handling your bitcoin.

Chapter 5. Best Exchanges for Trading Cryptocurrency

With the spiraling rise of cryptocurrency, we wanted to help you make the best choices when trading. Here is a list of all the exchanges for trading cryptocurrency based on their fees and features.

Coinbase

High liquidity so you can get in and out of your currency without slippage. It also allows for dollar deposits (rather than just credit card purchases). Coinbase has an affiliate program that partners with other companies to provide discounts on various goods or services. There is a hefty $3.5 billion funding, which means that Coinbase's management team may be better prepared to weather any potential storms. Coinbase charges a 0.25% fee on all transactions in terms of fees, and there are no customer service fees to speak of.

Currently, Coinbase is the most popular exchange for cryptocurrency trading in U.S. dollars. They charge a 1% fee for trades and purchases made via debit or credit card but do not charge anything for trades done using bank transfers. E-toro is excellent because you don't need to deposit money before your first trade, and it has the lowest commissions compared to other exchanges on this list at 0.1%.

To use Coinbase to buy cryptocurrency, you need to create an account. You need to be at least 18 years of age and live in a country where Coinbase operates.

Coinbase also offers web and mobile access for those without access to a computer or smartphone. If you are using coinbase through the web or the app, you will need to create an account before you can begin trading. You will need to verify your phone number via phone call and complete a short survey before being able to start trading.

Coinbase also offers free withdrawals; however, you will have to pay a fee when using a debit or credit card. The cryptocurrency price varies from payment to payment, but the USD withdrawal fee is about 5% for U.S. investors and 10% for international investors.

Coinbase also allows you to purchase Bitcoin with a linked bank account. You must wait until your bank transfers arrive in Coinbase before placing any trades. Coinjar offers faster deposits and withdrawals as it uses BitPay's high volume and low fee blockchain transaction processing platform on blockchain assets like Bitcoin. Bitfinex is another popular exchange to use as it has a large variety of payment methods, including bank transfers, SEPA bank transfers, and credit cards.

Coinbase is a highly trustworthy exchange that allows anyone with an email address to purchase cryptocurrencies without any verification, provided they only make small purchases. Robinhood, on the other hand, does not require any verification to trade cryptocurrencies. Still, all payments will be verified via your credit card processor, and if you are using your bank account, then your information will be verified via your bank.

Coinbase charges $1.49 per credit card transaction and $3.99 per bank transfer transaction, while Robinhood charges 2% for all top-ups, which can become very expensive for large purchases like Bitcoin or Ethereum.

Coinbase allows instant purchase and sales of cryptocurrency, but unlike Robinhood, they charge a fee for top-ups. Coinbase also has strict trading limits, and you will need verification before being allowed to trade over $25,000 in seven days.

Robinhood and Coinbase allow people living in the U.S., Europe, Canada, Australia, and Singapore to buy and sell cryptocurrencies freely. Still, it is unclear if these policies will change with time.

You can use Coinbase to purchase goods from companies like Tesla Motors, Virgin Galactic, Expedia, and Overstock if they accept cryptocurrencies as a form of payment.

Coinbase does have a clear-cut policy when it comes to cryptocurrencies, and that is "not to accept them as payment or sell them to people who want them as payment."

Coinbase allows for free withdrawals; however, all cryptocurrencies have to be sent back into Coinbase before being withdrawn because of their KYC policy. You will need to use your Coinbase address as your payment method when withdrawing funds from Coinbase, which can become complicated if you lose access to your account or if a hacker steals your login information.

E-Toro

E-Toro is one of the larger cryptocurrency trading platforms. The platform has a good selection of cryptocurrencies available, including Bitcoin and Ethereum, and also Bitcoin Cash and Ripple are being added later this year. eToro's fees are meager; trading commissions are charged only when you make a real profit rather than simply re-balancing your position, making the platform very cost-effective. Withdrawals can be made as often as you like, and it's possible to withdraw funds in USD or EUR.

To trade with E-toro, you will need to make a minimum deposit of $100 so that you can place the maximum allowable number of trades.

E-toro provides people with different ways to make their deposits, i.e., E-Toro through different ways, including bank transfers, credit cards, debit cards, PayPal, and SEPA bank transfers.

Robinhood

Robinhood is a new entrant into the cryptocurrency space, and they boast no trading fees whatsoever. This means that you can buy and sell Bitcoin (and Ethereum) without paying any transaction fees. The platform is relatively basic, with no margin trading or mobile app functionality, but it makes up for this by having some of the lowest fees in the industry.

Robinhood allows you to trade cryptocurrencies without paying any fees. Still, they do charge a premium for most Cryptocurrency purchases to cover the spread, which is essentially part of their "fee."

To get started buying cryptocurrency with Robinhood, you will have to create an account and fill out a short survey to verify your identity. During this process, permalink, it is essential that you use the same email address that you used when signing up for Coinbase because they will use this information to link your accounts.

Robinhood does not charge any fees for making deposits with a credit card, but it does charge a fee for trading, withdrawals, and transfers of Bitcoin and Ethereum which vary depending on which bank.

Robinhood allows you to deposit money in USD without any restrictions, but you will have to wait until your bank deposits before placing any trades.

Robinhood only charges a $5 deposit fee for those who use a debit or credit card to purchase a minimum of $100 and only charges fees when you trade cryptocurrency.

Coinmama

Coinmama is another more extensive cryptocurrency exchange that allows you to buy up to $150 or €150 worth of Bitcoin or Ether per day. Coinmama has a wide range of payment options, including credit card, which allows instant purchases of Bitcoin and Ether. Coinmama charges a -5% fee on credit card purchases.

Coinmama has the advantage of allowing most countries to use their service. Still, they have a few restrictions, and you must live in one of these countries: the United States, Canada, the European Union, United Kingdom, and many other European regions.

Coinmama allows you to buy Bitcoins with Cash in person using a VISA or MasterCard. You can also use a VISA/MasterCard, Paypal, or Credit Card for buying Bitcoins, but they do not accept cash in person or any other cryptocurrencies.

Coinmama's fees are also slightly higher than Coinbase, and they do not allow for any USD or cryptocurrency deposits before purchasing cryptocurrency.

Coinmama is also pretty similar to Coinbase in that you can only deposit money after making a purchase. However, with Coinmama, they offer several payment methods, including credit cards, debit cards, and Paypal.

BlockFi

BlockFi lets users buy Bitcoin through their FlexiCoin app, either by credit card or bank transfer. There is a 0.9% fee for buying Bitcoin, which is slightly higher than the competition.

BlockFi only charges $100 as its fee, but you will need to wait until your bank deposits before placing any trades.

To purchase cryptocurrency with BlockFi, you will have to sign up for an account before making any purchases. During the signup process, you will answer a few questions, and you will receive an email and a text message with your account number.

A common complaint with most of the exchanges on this list is that there are no limits to how many times you can deposit money. This can make it difficult to withdraw your money in case of an emergency.

Hodling

Hodling is a crypto-only investment service that doesn't allow you to trade cryptocurrencies but allows you to "hodl" your coins and earn interest on them over time. An all-inclusive set of fees means that they are across the industry as low as possible and include no management charges.

What is hodling? Hodl originated as a misspelling of the word "hold." In 2013, a BitcoinTalk forum user had wanted to type that he was no longer in the game of trading bitcoin but that he would hold his coins in the future.

He misspelled the word "hold" and wrote it as "hodl" instead. He made two attempts at correcting the spelling, but because he was drunk, he kept writing "hold" as "hodl."

The word "hodl" would get popular from that single event and become synonymous with holding bitcoin for a long time before selling.

When you hear someone say they are "hodling," it simply means they are holding bitcoin. It is a strategy for making a profit from bitcoin.

How it works is—you buy when the price is low, hodl until the price appreciates, and sell. The difference between the low price and the higher price becomes your profit.

It is one of the two ways of making money from crypto. The other method is trading which involves more skills and requires active involvement.

Hodling is more like a passive way of making money from crypto. However, it can go both ways–you may lose rather than gain.

Chapter 6. Getting Ready for Your Day Trading Career

Is Day Trading Right for You?

This is an important question you need to ask yourself.

Using the questions detailed above, you need to make sure you're going to be committed to becoming a day trader. You must understand you're going to be working long hours, and you don't precisely get holiday breaks since you're your boss and you're working for yourself.

You will also need to make sure you're not an emotionally reactive kind of person. It's guaranteed that you're going to invest in a stock at some point during your career, and you're going to lose money on it. That's just the way the game works, and it's inevitable.

However, if you're an emotional person and you lose a significant investment sum that causes you to freak out, you can bet you're going to make some bad decisions in the future. Likewise, there will be times when you win big money, and it's easy to get excited and want to invest more and make more. This is called greed and can backfire just as badly.

Being a day trader means being able to stand calm and relaxed in even the most stressful situations, remove emotion from your decision-making process, sticking to your plan, and remaining grounded. If you're not this sort of person, or you can't cultivate this kind of mindset, then day trading is probably not for you.

Setting Up Your Finances

Being able to manage your finances is vital before you set into the world of day trading. If you have any debt right now, you shouldn't even consider day trading until you've cleared it. If you have a loan or credit card, or both, where you're paying back interest rates of 20%, and you're only making a 5% return on your investments, then you're going to be losing money.

Instead, make sure you're paying off all your debts and then getting your capital ready. This way, you'll be minimizing how much interest you're paying on your credit and debt and then maximizing your profits when you start investing.

Once you're in the green, you need to start thinking about getting your capital in place. This is the starting amount of money you're going to be investing in. This can vary dramatically depending on your situation, so it's really up to you. You could start small, perhaps with $5,000, and then day trade part-time. As your capital grows over time, you can then begin transitioning over to becoming a full-time trader.

On the other hand, you may want to save up a lump sum that means you can quit your job and start investing straight away, although that's not recommended since you'll have no experience. Even if you have a lump sum, start small, so you can teach yourself the ropes of trading, and then start investing more and more once you start gathering experience.

Van Tharp, one of the top day traders in the world and author of Trade Your Way to Financial Freedom, recommends that if you're trading full-time, you're going to want around $100,000 to start with. If you're looking to day trade effectively, you're going to want approximately $10,000 in your trading account at all times.

The final financial aspect you'll want to consider is getting yourself a rainy-day emergency fund. This means creating a savings account where you put a recommended three months' worth of living expenses into an account and then leave it.

This means when you're trading, and if you ever come across a time in your life where you're suffering from financial difficulties, you'll have this fund to fall back on. However, it would help if you remembered this is not an account you can ever use for trading or investment. If you have a hard-losing streak and you need money to live on to support yourself and your family, you don't want to end up with anything. This is a financial crisis you'll want to avoid at all costs, which is why it's best to be as prepared as possible.

Learn About Stock Market Trading

This should go without saying, but if you want to become a day trader, you need to have some passion or interest in the stock market world or drive to become educated about it. You need to learn when the stock market trading hours are and how the processes and systems within the stock market work.

It would help if you had an interest in a particular niche or industry you want to trade in. You better have some passion surrounding it because you're going to need to be watching the news on this industry, reading news and books on the subjects, and investing your time watching interviews and learning about these stock market companies in terms of how they work and what they're up too daily.

You'll also need to learn about what stocks actually, as well as other potential trading options, such as ETFs, options, futures, and mutual funds. We'll briefly describe each one in the table below, but you must take time to develop a clear understanding of each other before you start implementing a trading strategy and investing in one.

- Stocks. When the ownership of a company or organization is broken down into all the shares, these are individually known as "stocks." Each stock represents fractional ownership of a company relative to the number of shares it has in total.

- ETFs. The term shortened for 'Exchanged-Traded Funds,' ETFs are a type of investment fund traded identically to a stock on the stock market and exchanges of the world. ETFs are indexes made of other securities and assets, such as stocks, special funds, and commodity funds.

- Options is the term given to a contract that gives a specific buyer a right to buy or sell any underlying asset, although it doesn't guarantee an obligation for sale. However, options will give the price that must be valid before or on a specified date stated on the option contract.

- Futures are another type of contract that points to the legal agreement that contracts the buying and selling of something at a price, time, and date that has been predetermined. However, these metrics won't be known by the parties involved and are classed as an asset.

- Mutual Funds. Mutual funds are investment portfolios that are managed by professional financial services. These services bring in money from several investors to buy stocks, shares, and other securities, like those in this table.

- Gold & Precious Metals. Gold (and sometimes other precious metals) refers to the trading asset of the metal gold stored in banks around the US and the world.

- Eminis are another type of futures contract that tracks the S&P 500 stock index market. It is also known as the E-Mini, ES, or just Mini.
- Cryptocurrency is a broad term that refers to the trade of cryptocurrencies within the stock market. This can be done individually or via an exchange.
- Forex is trading foreign currencies worldwide by converting one currency into another and then trading in this manner.

Practice Your Money Management Skills

The last thing you need to do before you even start to think about getting ready to trade stocks is to consider how practical your money management skills are. If you're thinking to yourself, "yeah, my money management skills are pretty good," then take a step back and consider how you can improve. There's always room to be better, and as a day trader, these are improvements you're going to both want and need.

Consider this. If you're starting with $100,000 and you're using a tried-and-tested strategy that has a 60% success rate, how much are you going to invest, to begin with? What happens if your first four trades fail and come out as a loss? How should you be allocating your capital?

With any trading, it's always a good idea to start small and then expand over time. It's rather stupid to jump in on your first trade and buy $100,000 worth of stock and hope for the best. Of course, it might pay off, but if you're this risky with your first investment, the chances are it's going to backfire dramatically later down the line.

Work on your money management skills and nurture the ability to step back and make decisions from a grounded state of mind. You need to wisely select which opportunities you're going to invest in and how you're going to manage your investment capital. Even if you're using a 30% success rate strategy, you can still make a large amount of profit from it when you have proper money management skills.

Once you've developed all these aspects of your life and got yourself ready, you're one step closer to starting your day trading career. Before we jump into the meat of what you need to do and start investing, there's one more aspect we need to cover, and that's developing your day trading mindset.

Why Do You Trade?

Answer: It's simple—the only reason to trade is to make money! This question, why do you trade, is essential and something to think about as we conclude this topic.

While the answer "to make money" might seem obvious—a no-brainer—most losing traders, actually trade for other reasons. They may think they are trading to make money, but their actions indicate that other motivations drive their decisions. Remember, the most critical indicator is you.

If you are genuinely trading to make money, then the next logical question to ask is how… How does a trader achieve that objective?

The answer is by trading within the context and rules of a proven trade plan. A proven trade plan grows equity in your account, despite the random distribution of wins and losses. It includes rules to follow that you can prove to yourself.

Taking random trades that are not within the context of a proven trade plan is not trading to make money. It is something else. Why? Because we are traders. It is what we do. We take trades. If you win on a random trade, now what? There is still another trade to take. Making money comes from the edge that your proven trade plan gives you over time. Random trades are not going to reveal whether or not you have an edge—they're random—until after the fact, when you will most likely learn that the answer is no, you did not have an edge. And then it will be too late. This is how accounts get blown up.

If you are genuinely trading to make money, then your actions should reflect that. If they do not, you will most likely trade for other reasons that you don't quite understand. You will need to address that if you genuinely want to internalize the right reason to trade, make money. Otherwise, the market will give you something else, and you probably will not like it.

Chapter 7. How to Buy

Most of the time, buying Bitcoin is a relatively straightforward process. The only problem is that not a lot of people know how and where to start. In this chapter, I will guide you through buying Bitcoin and other related cryptocurrencies and what you need to make the buying process even easier on your part.

Before You Begin….

To start things off, there are several things that you need to get sorted out first before you start buying Bitcoin. Here are some of the essentials that every Bitcoin Buyer/Investor would need:

An account at a cryptocurrency exchange

- A digital wallet (more on this later)
- Personal identification documents if you opt for a Know Your Customer Policy
- A strong internet connection
- A chosen payment method

For your payment method, you have several options, including your bank account, a debit card, and credit cards. There are also specialized payment methods designed for Bitcoin and other P2P exchanges. However, keep in mind that some Bitcoin-centric ATMs are starting to require government-issued IDs to be registered, so get your documents sorted out first.

Aside from your essential documents, we also need to work on your attitude. The key to success with Bitcoin is privacy and security. As such, it is highly recommended that you rein in any tendency to flap your gums and brag about your holdings.

If you get the private key to the address of a Bitcoin blockchain, you have the power to authorize transactions. This key should be kept secret as criminals would do their best to get a hold of that to secure all the information held in that blockchain.

Your patience is also a necessary trait. Although transactions are instantaneous, it takes a while before you get the hang of the system and start earning from your investments. Do not enter into the trade just for short-term benefits. There have been countless times when buyers and investors ventured into trading at the worst possible time, quit, and gain a negative perception of the entire market.

You have to stick it out and see where things go next. As such, this patience must also be accompanied by a bit of caution. You cannot be reckless with your decisions here, nor can you overspend on one currency. Have a plan, and do your best to stick to that. The less you go off the script, the more likely it will be for you to earn quite a lot with Bitcoin.

Aside from these, there are also four other considerations that you must always keep in mind before you start buying cryptocurrencies.

1. Volatility is the Norm, Not the Exception

Remember that the prices of cryptocurrencies are still known for their dramatic shifts in both directions, even in recent years. In fact, in 2017 alone, the value of Bitcoin went from $900.00 to $2,000.00.

That sounds good. Not exactly.

That only tells you that things can change in the market at the drop of a dime. One change can cause the prices to go upwards or downwards, depending on the situation. You so much as sneeze, and the costs for cryptocurrencies can change dramatically.

Sure, volatility is a recurring feature in most commodities, but they do not feature periodic massive spikes in the trend every month. That being said, don't get too reckless when you venture into the market.

2. Cryptocurrencies Still Have a Lot of Unknown Variables

As of now, there are still a lot of kinks that need to be ironed out when it comes to cryptocurrencies. That could be the reason why prices are fluctuating since everybody is still scrambling to know what to do with the entire concept

Only a few people have a better grasp of how things work in the market, not even the complete picture. This means that you should learn all that you can about how things work in the market before you start buying crypto coins. Hopefully, you should have considerable knowledge of the market as of this point.

3. Fraud Is Still a Problem

Due to the anonymity being offered by cryptocurrencies, many people have taken advantage of the system and used it for many dubious activities. The term cryptocurrencies were synonymous with black market deals for quite a while in the 2010s before things started stabilizing by the end of the decade.

That being said, just be prepared for a lot of risks when it comes to this market.

4. There Is (Still) No Proper Standard ROI

Many experts recommend that you treat investments less of a gamble and more of an informed purchase. But, with the many unknown variables, cryptocurrencies tend to fit the bill of the former than the latter. There is no standard pattern to predict rises and falls, there is not enough data, and there are not enough credible sources to draw information.

This means that nobody can tell you that there is a healthy ROI when it comes to cryptocurrencies. Sure, some may have made it big with Bitcoin, but there is still insufficient data to support that vast payouts are a 100% certainty here.

With all these considerations of the way, it is now time that we start learning how to purchase your first virtual coins.

Step 1: Knowing Where to Buy

Where do you buy Bitcoin? The short answer is an exchange. Also, you can trade, sell, and hold cryptocurrencies with the sale of your choice so pay attention to this part correctly. The general rule is that you must pick an exchange that allows for transfers into a wallet. This is so you could better safeguard your investments. Sadly, not all sales and broker agencies offer this option.

Also, keep in mind that each exchange does offer its unique perk. Some allow you to remain anonymous by not requiring you to present personal information. Other deals provide central banking services, especially in regions where their banking system is not reliable.

The point is that there is an exchange out there that might fit your needs. Here are some that are considered to be the best in the industry right now.

A. Coinbase

Advantages of Coinbase

- Beginner-friendly UI
- High rate of liquidity

Disadvantages of Coinbase

- High fees if you don't use Coinbase Pro
- No control over the wallet keys
- Comparatively fewer currency options than other exchanges

Founded in 2012, Coinbase is perhaps one of the first crypto exchanges out there. It has a license to operate in the United States and 40 other territories globally and has generally remained controversy-free.

What makes Coinbase attractive is its platform that is easy to understand and use. Since you are new, you should get the hang of the market using this exchange.

The wallets in Coinbase are also insured, although such insurance does not apply if the mistake could be attributed to your recklessness. Also, a Pro option offers cheaper fees and more options to track currency performances in the market.

As for the regular fees, Coinbase offers them at $0.99 to $2.99 depending on the dollar value of each purchase.

B. Cash App

Advantages of Cash App

- P2P money transfers
- Bitcoin withdrawal feature
- Simple UI

Disadvantages of Cash App

- Exclusive to Bitcoin (for now)
- 3% charge if you send money using a credit card
- $2,000 Daily Withdrawal Limit

Considered to be one of the better apps for beginners, Cash App is essentially a peer-to-peer money transfer system that allows you to perform several transactions. That includes paying for rent.

What makes Cash App great is its simplicity. It acts like a bank account that allows for different transactions and even the holding of credit. However, Cash App also functions as a platform where you could invest in stocks and cryptocurrencies.

Also, Cash App allows you to withdraw any cryptocurrency you might have stored on the platform. This is because the App will enable you to take possession of the keys that unlock your coins.

As of now, Cash App charges a fee for every transaction that you make. Also, the prices can change depending on the volatility of the market and other external factors.

C. Binance

Advantages of Binance

- Comparatively lower transaction fees
- One of the largest selections of altcoins.
- Advanced charting systems.

Disadvantages of Binance

- A bit too advanced for beginners.

Binance is a relatively strong contender in the worldwide cryptocurrency market as transactions occurring in its platform make up a considerable portion of the worldwide volume for market activity. It may not exactly allow you to deposit US Dollars, but Binance allows for coin purchases using your debit cards and other international currencies.

As such, this platform is great if you are living outside of the United States and are interested in investing in lesser-known yet still competitive cryptocurrencies. And if you have a hang with charting, Binance does allow for more options of performance indexes. On paper, this should help you identify precisely where a particular coin is performing the strongest and in what market.

For fees, know that Binance takes 0.1% for the buyer and another 0.1% on the seller for every transaction made. There are also other fees to be charged when you use the other services of Binance. But with the BNB coins, those fees can be reduced by 25% every transaction.

D. Bisq

Advantages of Bisq

- Decentralized system
- Non-KYC policies
- Optimized for mobile devices

Disadvantages of Bisq

- Slow transaction speeds highly likely regardless of native Internet connection speeds.
- Low trading volumes depending on the region.
- Not suited for active traders.

Although many deride Bisq's open accessibility as a potential security issue, the platform more than makes up for it with its fully decentralized system. This means that there is no central point of possible failure within the system. To put it simply, if one part gets compromised, the other nodes can isolate it and continue functioning as if nothing happened.

Aside from this, Bisq is sought after for its accessibility. You can choose to do your trading on a desktop/laptop PC or a mobile device, and the rate of success for each transaction remains at a constant high.

As of now, Bisq accepts fiat currencies and a sizeable number of cryptocurrencies like Bitcoin. If you use the native coin, BSQ, fees are either reduced or free for your transactions. If you don't, the platform takes 0.10% on the maker's side and 0.70% on the side of the take for each transaction.

Chapter 8. How to Trade

Hopefully, now that you've bought a Bitcoin let's go to the next step because once the Bitcoin settles into your account, there are two different paths that you can take. Either the cold route or my personal favorite, the hot route, and what I mean by that is that you can keep your Bitcoin on the exchange itself, and that's considered a hot wallet. The benefit of doing this is that you have immediate liquidity because your Bitcoin can be sold right away, exchanged for another coin, or made to earn interest on another website, all of which are fantastic. However, the disadvantage is that you must trust that those exchanges or businesses will keep your money safe from computer hackers attempting to steal it. The second option is to use cold storage, which involves taking our coins offline and transferring them to the blockchain using the Ledger Nano wallet.

But first, I'd like to show you the hot wallet route, which is what I use because I believe your money should be earning interest and making you passive income on a consistent basis, so what I like to use is BlockFi. If you decide to go this route, please carefully follow the next few steps.

Go to the top of the website and look for "deposit," which you can click and then choose the coin you purchased from the brokerage. I'm going to use Bitcoin as an example, so that's what I'd go with, and there's a link at the bottom. That is your wallet's public address. By pressing on a portion of the page icon, you can copy that number and paste it into your brokerage. Returning to Gemini, if you go to transfer then withdraw from Gemini, you can choose the currency and then the destination, which is where you paste the BlockFi code. Then you'll want to choose the amount you want to send and double-check that your wallet address in Gemini matches what it shows in BlockFi, because if any digit is off, your money will disappear under the table. You don't want that because it will never return. It will be the most stressful few minutes of your life once you send the money over. Please exercise extreme caution. You won't know if you did it correctly for the next few minutes, so send a small amount first to ensure that you got the process right and don't send the entire balance over and lose it, and then send the rest of the amount. The concept of earning interest in cryptocurrency is not unique to BlockFi. Also available are the Celsius network and Nexo.io. I like BlockFi because it integrates well with Gemini, and the majority of the money on BlockFi is kept in a Gemini cold storage wallet. The two have teamed up on this, and another reason I trust BlockFi is that you can see all of the money backing them on their investor relations page. This venture capital money is significant and well-respected in the industry, and I trust that they are making the best decisions possible. If BlockFi goes away, not only will it make them look bad, but it will also make the investors look bad, which is why I chose BlockFi. But don't just use the same companies I do; I'd like you to try something new.I want to give you as many options as possible.

If you're thinking to yourself, "This is still far too complicated," and you want to keep your Bitcoin on the exchange, know that you're still taking on unnecessary risk without benefiting from the interest. Send your money to a cold storage offline wallet instead if you're going to do that. This virtually guarantees that your money will be kept in the safest possible location, which is on the blockchain, which no one has yet been able to break into. So, let me explain hardware wallets a little bit more. It's a $57 device that you can get directly from Ledger, but you should get one as soon as your cryptocurrency balance reaches $1,000. On the Ledger website, there are many tutorials for getting this device up and running, and once you get it, it will give you a list of key phrases and words to write down and hide somewhere. Never take a photo of these keywords, never upload them, and never have someone else do it for you. Not a fiduciary, a tax expert, or a banker, because anyone who knows your list of key phrases can open your wallet at any time and steal your money. As soon as you write that down, put it somewhere safe and forget about it, because as long as you have your secret list, you'll be able to access your Bitcoin even if your hardware wallet is lost or destroyed. Another reason I don't recommend using Robinhood to buy crypto is that you can't remove your coins and deposit them somewhere like this. If you've ever bought, sold, or exchanged Bitcoin, you'll almost certainly have to pay taxes on it. Here's how you can do so automatically now that you're a crypto expert and know everything there is to know about Bitcoin. I use Taxbit, and there are a few others, but this one is great because it integrates almost every account automatically. You grant these websites access to your cryptocurrency accounts, but they are unable to make any changes. They are unable to purchase, sell, or steal them. It's just an auditing position. You can give them an auditor role by going to settings and selecting API under programmatic access in Gemini's case. They'll be able to enter automatically after that. They calculate all of your purchases and sales, and it simply aggregates everything for you. You can then print out that sheet, give it to your accountant, and everything will be calculated automatically.

Chapter 9. How to Invest

There are some things you should know as a beginner before diving into cryptocurrency investing so that you can get off to a good start, sleep well at night, and manage your crypto assets like a boss!

Because cryptocurrencies are a high-risk investment, never invest more than you can afford to lose as a beginner. Yes, it will be tempting to use all of your money to buy some currencies at a certain point in time, especially if the market sector offers a window of opportunity and the price of a particular currency falls. Always remember that you should never invest more money than you can afford to lose.

Cryptocurrency usage varies. There are many different currencies that are used for various purposes. Although it is a common belief that cryptocurrencies are only used for illegal transactions and business. This is untrue!

Cryptocurrencies can be used for a wide range of purposes, as even some of the world's most successful business people use them for their transactions. Cryptocurrency, on the other hand, is notorious for funding theft and illegal transactions. Legitimate businesses, on the other hand, accept cryptocurrency payments. So cryptocurrency cannot be categorized solely by its negative aspects, and it should not be labeled as illegal because it is also a legal means of exchange.

Cryptocurrency helps you save both time and money. In fact, transferring 99 million dollars in Litecoin (LTC) took only two and a half minutes, and the sender paid fewer transaction fees as a result. Without a doubt, cryptocurrency is one of the simplest and fastest ways to send large sums of money to any location on the planet. You can send the currency from the comfort of your bed while sipping tea once you have all the information you require from the other person. Isn't it cool? Yeah.

Emotions can have an impact on cryptocurrency prices. Throughout history, asset-class bubbles have occurred numerous times. From the Dutch tulip bulb mania in the 1600s to the dot-com bubble in the 2000s, various popular assets have been bid up by enthusiastic investors in the past. FOMO is a term used frequently by investors (Fear Of Missing Out). Because of the hype from other investors, this fear causes many cryptocurrency investors to enter the investing trend at an inopportune time.

Calculating the intrinsic value of cryptocurrency for a publicly traded company may be more difficult. However, even though it may be tempting, learning about several assets and how well they perform may help you avoid investing at its peak. So, if you want to dive deep into cryptocurrency, you'll need more industry knowledge and a better understanding of the digital currency market to become a more informed cryptocurrency investor.

Understand that you are your own bank before investing in cryptocurrency. When it comes to cryptocurrencies, you and only you have control over your funds; no one else is in charge of them. Unlike traditional banking systems, we have a fully functional system for saving your money and handling your numerous transactions. This is something you don't have with cryptocurrency. You may be concerned as a result of this, but rest assured that being your bank has its advantages, one of which is that you are not overcharged for every transaction you make on your account.

You can also choose to create a wallet from anywhere in the world without having to enter a building or wait in long lines! Although, as your bank, you have the right to keep your currencies secure and your device free of hackers and viruses. You're ready to go once you've secured your wallets. You should be aware that while trading on your cryptocurrency account, you are not anonymous. The public has access to all bitcoin transactions. Every bitcoin purchased or spent is visible to your fellow investors. So you should be aware that anyone who has your bitcoin address (likely someone you traded with) can check all of your previous transactions.

Chapter 10. How to Protect

On this page, I'll show you step by step how to get started investing in Bitcoin, how to keep it safe and secure, how to earn some passive income and interest with it, and, most importantly, how to pay your taxes with it automatically, because that's something you should know. Because the cryptocurrency space isn't known for being the most ethical, I want to make sure that no one is taken advantage of because, no matter what you tell them, half the world believes Bitcoin is a scam. Don't offend the other half, who believe it's about religion. I'm in the middle because I believe that investing all of your money in it is a bad idea, but I also believe that investing none of your money is a bad idea. Bitcoin has been around for over ten years and has stood up to every technological test we've put it through. We still don't know what's around the corner, and despite the fact that Bitcoin is likely to be the most valuable and promising cryptocurrency, the technology is bound to be disrupted in the future. I believe Bitcoin will be around for a long time, but only invest what you are comfortable with.

First and foremost, use the best brokerage. The answer is dependent on what you value most. That means safety and security, ease of use, and value for me, so I want to make sure that the money I invest is, first and foremost, extremely secure. Second, I want to ensure that the interface does not appear overly complicated. Third, I want to make sure I'm getting good value and not overpaying in fees. I'm willing to pay a little more for an extra layer of security. Whatever brokerage you choose, two things are required: AML and KYC. Know Your Customer and Anti-Money Laundering regulations must be followed. That means they'll all need your ID, address, phone number, and any other information required by standard brokerage. Gemini and Coinbase are my two favorite brokerages. Both are fantastic, and I have accounts with both. You can't go wrong with either, and the signup process is nearly identical. However, the less information you give them, the lower your limit for buying and selling Bitcoin will be. Your limit will increase as you provide more information.

Because Gemini is the brokerage I use the most, I'll describe how the signup process works there. Your first name, last name, email address, and password will be requested first, followed by your phone number.

Following that, it will request a passport photo or a driver's license ID, as well as a passport number and a physical mailing address. You're good to go once you've finished that. After you've signed up for the next step, make sure your account is safe and secure so that no one can steal your Bitcoins. You can do this by downloading the free app "authy" from the app store. This is to ensure that even if someone has our username, email, and passwords, they won't be able to log in and do anything malicious unless they have physical access to our phone, which they hopefully don't. Gemini should automatically appear in the app after you've downloaded "authy." You can click on it to reveal a seven-digit number that will recycle every 20 seconds countinously. After that, Gemini will ask for the seven-digit number on a regular basis to ensure it's you, but once you're satisfied, we can move on to the next step. First, you must fund your account, and Coinbase offers a variety of ways to do so, including credit cards. However, you should never buy Bitcoin with a credit or debit card because the fees are ridiculously high at 3.49 percent. That's high because, for comparison, the stock market returns 7% per year, and you'll only have to pay half of that to begin investing. Never pay more than 3.49 percent for anything. Connect your bank account instead. There are two ways to do it: the manual way, where they send you pennies and you confirm ownership of your bank account with them, or the easier way, which is to go to the upper right-hand corner, click on "account settings," then "funding sources," and then click on the "automatically link bank account" option. This connects everything automatically using a third-party software integration, and these brokerages do not have access to your bank accounts. It's only possible through "plaid," a highly secure and safe service. I've connected two accounts, but doing it manually will take a few days versus using "plaid," which is almost instantaneous. This is how you can transfer money from your bank into your brokerage once you've connected your funding sources. After that, go to Gemini and click on transfer. You'll be prompted to choose a currency at this point. You can simply use the United States dollar. You'll see two deposit methods: bank transfer and wire transfer. The bank transfer option limits you to $15,000 per day, which should cover most people, but if you're doing more than that, you'll have to use the wire transfer option. When you hit continue, a list of instructions will appear, but the reference code is something you should pay attention to. This tells Gemini which account to deposit your money into, ensuring that your money does not end up in the wrong hands. That is your one-of-a-kind identifierYou won't use a wire transfer if you're from Europe. You'll use the Sepa transfer, and if you're Canadian, you'll use PayPal to withdraw your money and then use debit cards to buy it, which isn't the best option, but it'll suffice. Let's buy some Bitcoin now that you've funded your account. On the front page, you can see all of the different currencies you can invest in, but Bitcoin and Ethereum should be your primary concerns. They are the most legitimate projects in this space, having been the first, and having the best future growth potential. If you wanted to buy Bitcoin, all you had to do was click on it on this page. Then you can choose to buy it once, daily, weekly, or monthly, and you can enter the amount based on how much you want to invest, and then click "view order," where you can enter the payment method and choose which one you want, and then place the order. That's it. Before we move on to the next step, there's something I want you to know about the next section. If you think you're going to become a millionaire overnight with Bitcoin and then cash out, there are a few things you should be aware of. If you wanted to buy Bitcoin, all you had to do was click on it on this page. Then you can choose to buy it once, daily, weekly, or monthly, and you can enter the amount based on how much you want to invest, and then click "view order," where you can enter the payment method and choose which one you want, and then place the order. That's it. Before we move on to the next step, there's something I want you to know about the next section. If you think you're going to become a millionaire overnight with Bitcoin and then cash out, there are a few things you should be aware of.

Chapter 11. Trading Bots

So, what exactly are cryptocurrency trading bots? They're basically computer programs that trade on your behalf based on a set of instructions or rules. So, if a certain price target is met, you might buy X amount of Bitcoin. When that rule is met, the bots will execute the trade you requested automatically. This means that in order to use a crypto trading bot, you must first connect it to a crypto exchange account via an API, or application program interface. That API allows your trading BOTS to place trades at the exchange programmatically. As a result, you'll be able to trade while sleeping. You're essentially giving a computer program access to your exchange account. What if the bot's code is compromised, or the company that created the crypto BOTS turns out to be a scam? All of these are legitimate concerns that you should be aware of. Will your Binance account be taken over by machines? Well, not quite. The good news is that exchange API permissions can be set. You can choose what specific API keys in your account can do. You can only choose to write buy or sell orders in the crypto trading BOT, not to initiate a withdrawal. Probably a good idea. You can also set IP address restrictions. That means that any instructions must originate from your IP address, which is a clever way to guard against a fraudulent crypto trading bot. Trends come and go on a regular basis. A bot is not a replacement for a knowledgeable trader. You must keep your funds on an exchange in order to use them. Although there are many reputable and secure businesses out there, hacks do occur. After that, I'll go over some of the best and most well-known cryptocurrency trading bots. Shrimpy is a social portfolio management tool and cryptocurrency trading platform that debuted in 2018 and quickly grew in popularity among traders. The value proposition was straightforward. Provide as many top-of-the-line trading tools as possible at the most affordable price. As a result, they provide a wide range of free services. It's worth noting that Shrimpy isn't intended for use as a signal or indicator. As a result, it is not an ideal tool for day traders. Instead, it's a long-term portfolio management tool Rebalancing, dollar-cost averaging, and stop-loss orders are all automated. KuCoin, Binance, Coinbase, GEMINI, OKEX, Bitfinex, Poloniex, BITtrex, BitMart, and Huobi Global are among the exchanges that support the Shrimpy crypto trading bot. What does all of this cost? Shrimpie, on the other hand, has a fairly comprehensive free plan that allows you to link an unlimited number of exchanges to track your portfolio's performance, blacklist assets, access an asset balance tracker, and more. You'll need to upgrade to a paid plan if you want to automate portfolio management, backtest trading strategies, or use Shrimpie social trading features. If you choose the annual plan, it will cost you only $13 per month, or $19 per month if you pay monthly. Shrimpie also has a business plan available.

With over 45,000 active users, 14,000 active trading BOTS, and 1.8 million completed trades, TradeSanta is a cloud-based BOT with a solid reputation. I do, however, want to issue a fair warning. Some of the features may take some time to become accustomed to. When it comes to features, TradeSanta offers a long bot template to use when you expect a crypto asset's price to rise, a short bot template to use when you expect it to fall, and a custom template to use when you want to use the bot's full functionality. Aside from that, TradeSanta provides you with an abundance of technical indicators to analyze cheval cheval cheval cheval cheval cheval cheval cheval cheval cheval cheval cheval cheval cheval cheval cheval cheval Bollinger signals, trade filters, and volume filters are examples of these types of filters. Real-time tracking is another useful feature, allowing you to keep track of the bot's progress on the go using transparent analytics and telegram notifications. An iOS and Android app is also available for TradeSanta. HitBTC, Binance, BitMEX, Houbi, OKEX, Bitfinex, and

BITtrex are among the exchanges supported by TradeSanta. The good news in terms of pricing is that TradeSanta offers a five-day free trial. So go ahead and poke around with the bot to see if it's worth your hard-earned cash. After that, you can use the free version, which allows you to use only two bots and has a monthly volume limit of $3,000 per month. You'll also have unlimited access to trading pairs, all TradeSanta strategies, telegram notifications, and general customer support. The basic plan includes everything that the basic program does, plus access to up to 49 BOTS and the ability to run an unlimited amount of trade volume through the bot. This will cost you $14 per month. This is the plan I recommend to most people who use TradeSanta. You can, however, upgrade to the popular BTC promo plan for an additional $7 per month. This plan includes everything in the basic plan as well as 0% trading fees on HitBTC. Some may argue that this is a valuable benefit, but I'm not a big fan of HitBTC The top pay plan on TradeSanta includes everything in the basic plan, plus 0% trading fees on HitBTC and access to an unlimited number of bots. This will cost you $70 per month. To be honest, I doubt any of you will need to pay $70 per month.

Crypto Hopper offers expert trading tools without requiring coding knowledge. If you are interested in more advanced trading techniques such as market making and exchange arbitrage, this bot is for you. There are also many trading templates, strategies, and signals to choose from in the Crypto Hopper marketplace. These signals enable you to subscribe to professional analysts all over the world, and Crypto Hopper trades with them. However, keep in mind that not everything in the marketplace is free. If you want to access your trading bot while you're on the go, there's an Android and iOS app for that. Crypto Hopper integrates with the following crypto exchanges: KuCoin, Binance, Coinbase, OKEX, Bitfinex, Poloniex, BITtrex, HitBTC Kraken, and Huobi Global. In terms of pricing, Crypto Hopper provides a seven-day free trial. The basic pan costs $16 per month and is suitable for the majority of day traders. If you want to do exchange arbitrage, you'll have to pay $41 per month, and the market-making license will cost you $83 per month. What are the bot's benefits and drawbacks? On the plus side, it is simple to set up and inexpensive. The market is fantastic, and coin and exchange support is excellent. My only complaint is that I couldn't see who was behind the bot. Transparency is essential in the crypto world. Who can benefit from Crypto Hopper? To be honest, almost anyone would be interested in using a high-quality cryptocurrency bot at a reasonable cost.

Gunbot, also known as Gun-T. It's a popular crypto bot that runs on Mac, Windows, and Linux, so you can use it on almost any computer. When it comes to features, Gunbot has numerous inbuilt trading strategies such as step game, gain, and ping pong. Another cool feature of Gunbot is the ability to customize your trading strategies, and the bot will execute those trades for you. When it comes to mobile support, Gunbot is fairly well optimized. Gunbot also works with a large number of top-tier exchanges, including Coinbase Pro and margin trading on BITmex, Kraken, and OKEX. This one, however, differs from the others in that it is subscription-based. Gunbot instead charges a one-time license fee. The cost of the starter pack is 0.02 Bitcoin. However, Gunbot will only allow you to trade on one supporter exchange and access free trading strategies. Gunbot standard gives you access to all trading strategies, but you can only use the bot once. This will cost you 0.05 Bitcoin. Gunbot Pro is where things start to heat up in terms of pricing. It will cost you 0.075 Bitcoin, but you will be able to use the bot on three different exchanges and gain access to trading strategy backtesting. The bot also has a variety of add-ons and upgrades.

Crypto Hopper offers expert trading tools without requiring coding knowledge. If you are interested in more advanced trading techniques such as market making and exchange arbitrage, this bot is for you.

There are also many trading templates, strategies, and signals to choose from in the Crypto Hopper marketplace. These signals enable you to subscribe to professional analysts all over the world, and Crypto Hopper trades with them. However, keep in mind that not everything in the marketplace is free. If you want to access your trading bot while you're on the go, there's an Android and iOS app for that. Crypto Hopper integrates with the following crypto exchanges: KuCoin, Binance, Coinbase, OKEX, Bitfinex, Poloniex, BITtrex, HitBTC Kraken, and Huobi Global. In terms of pricing, Crypto Hopper provides a seven-day free trial. The basic pan costs $16 per month and is suitable for the majority of day traders. If you want to do exchange arbitrage, you'll have to pay $41 per month, and the market-making license will cost you $83 per month.

3commas is one of the most popular BOTS, with over 140,000 users and a daily trade volume of $65 million. It has an extremely user-friendly interface that is jam-packed with detailed analytics and a plethora of functions. You can also use the bot to set stop loss and take profit targets and create trading strategies. I particularly appreciate 3commas' smart trading functionality. For example, you could use Bitcoin to purchase Ethereum. However, when performing an audit on some exchanges, you must decide whether to set a profit or a stop loss. You can't always set both, which is inconvenient. However, with three commas, you can easily and quickly set trailing stop losses. That is, if the market rises by 5%, the trailing stop loss increases your stop-loss by 5%. Some exchanges allow you to set profit levels and stop losses at the same time, but if the trading pair you want to trade isn't available, you don't have to miss out on the opportunity. Furthermore, 3commas provides backtesting, dollar cost averaging BOTS, a plethora of trading tools, a traders diary to keep track of all your trades, and a highly developed signals marketplace that allows you to mimic and automate the transactions provided by the top signals providers. That means you can simply follow the signals and let the bot do the heavy lifting. 3commas has not overlooked mobile users.

Chapter 12. Leverage

So you have a budget set aside for trading, but you now also need to be responsible for how you manage your risk. Another widespread mistake I see traders make is using way too much leverage. Leverage is a double-edged sword. It can enhance your gains, but it can also chop you down to size. Placing trades with a narrow margin down means that one unforeseen swing in the market could wipe out your trading account. This is particularly relevant in the cryptocurrency markets where you're trading incredibly volatile assets. Bitcoin has many mood swings, and a negative move can leave you with less than half your money. Leverage to that, and the losses are even more severe.

Moreover, there's no reason whatsoever for you to max out your leverage. Just because you can trade with 100 times your capital does not mean you should. You can be just as successful in the long run using the leverage of even less than 20 times. A well-thought-out money management strategy overlaid with a carefully crafted risk management strategy is the most effective way to stay in the game even in the bad times.

Leverage Trading

What is leverage trading, exactly? Simply put, it's when you trade with more money than you have. To elaborate, it entails taking market positions that are many times the amount of collateral you're putting down. This collateral is more commonly referred to as your margin, and it is usually expressed as a percentage of your trading capital. For example, if the margin is 20% of the position, it implies a five-fold leverage. A ten percent margin implies ten times leverage. This means that a specific factor influences your position. The said factor magnifies gains and losses. This quality of leverage trading can make it profitable or deadly, depending on which side of the trade you are on. Leveraged trading is quite broad, and various instruments can provide leverage. To trade, you can use Financial Futures, Swap Instruments, CFDs (Contracts for Difference), or even pure Margin Borrowing. Another feature of some of these leverage instruments is their ability to be used to short sell an asset. This means you'll be able to profit from a decrease in the value of the asset. That is a basic overview of leverage instruments, but we will look at their history in traditional finance to better understand their role in crypto markets. Futures contracts are almost as old as finance itself; they were first used centuries ago as a way for farmers to hedge the risk of forwarding commodity prices. They would sell their product in the future to lock in a price when it hit the market. After a few decades, these instruments were tradable on large exchanges like the CME or Chicago Mercantile Exchange. They were no longer just a product to help farmers and buyers hedge their risks; they were also used to speculate on commodity prices. Who wants to make predictions about soybeans and orange juice? In the early 1970s, futures markets were extended to currency markets. Interest rate markets in 1975 and stock market indices in the 1980s By mm, you had futures instruments on individual stocks as well. These were mostly traded by institutional investors on large regulated exchanges like the CME and CBOE. Those traders would maintain margin accounts with exchange members who required less than the contract's notional size. These margin accounts are quite high, implying a leverage of only three to five times. However, the fact that futures were not made available to retail traders is significant. The risks associated with trading them were, indeed, relatively high. Losses could be multiples of the margin, and retail investors were not thought to be knowledgeable about trading these financial products. These eventually made their way into retail markets via the numerous online brokerage accounts available to US traders. Futures and margin borrowing were no longer limited to institutional investors. However, depending on the asset, leverage limits have remained between 5 and 20 times. It's also worth noting that the US Securities and Exchange Commission closely monitors these brokers.

Chapter 13. Fundamental Analysis

Fundamental analysis is also called the lifeblood of investment. The key to using it is to gather as much information and facts as possible. It stands on the premise that the more you understand a particular cryptocurrency, the more likely it is to predict its price movement in the market. Hence, when you use fundamental analysis, you should follow the latest news. The news has a powerful influence on the price of a cryptocurrency.

To give you an idea: when CNN featured just how high the price of Bitcoin was increasing at that time, it further pushed the price of Bitcoin upward. When China declared that it would close down all its cryptocurrency exchanges, the price of Bitcoin and other cryptocurrencies dropped. When Russia removed its ban on the use of Bitcoins and other cryptocurrencies, the price of Bitcoin experienced a significant increase in value. As you can see, by being aware of the latest news and analyzing its implications in the market, you can get a good idea of how the price of specific cryptocurrencies will most likely be affected.

News is not the only source of information. You should also check the white paper released by the developer of a cryptocurrency. Although it may be hard to understand due to the technical terms, it will provide you with helpful information regarding the cryptocurrency.

You should also join related online groups and forums. Many developers are active in these places, which will allow you to get information from the developers, but you can also even contact them if you want. You can also learn from the other members of the cryptocurrency community. From time to time, you will surely come across exciting points of view and valuable strategies that you can use to make a profit in the cryptocurrency market.

This tool is essential because it deals with the basics. If you do not understand the basics, how do you think you can make the right investment decision otherwise? Therefore, always do your research and analysis of the different cryptocurrencies in the market. Do not be lazy.

Fundamental analysis can be used with other tools. People usually use this tool together with technical analysis. If you consider yourself a trustworthy and professional cryptocurrency investor/trader, you must use it, regardless of other tools you may want to use. After all, if you do not know the fundamentals, it would be hard to think of yourself as a fundamental investor/trader.

Chapter 14. Technical Analysis

The cryptocurrency market is undoubtedly filled with lots of uncertainties and volatilities. Traders are always urged to analyze the market before delving in carefully. In light of this, traders adopt different strategies and techniques to beat the market and make huge profits. Which one works depends on a few factors, including your forbearance for risk, commitment, and so on. In the end, the onus lies in the circumstances of individuals.

There is no one-size-fits-all in terms of trading cryptocurrencies. Remember that it is very pertinent to do your research correctly before exploring the market. Also never, invest more than you are willing to lose. None of these tactics is foolproof, and there is a certain amount of risk associated with any trading.

Furthermore, trading tactics are specific or rather iconic to certain individuals and may not be generalized. For the avoidance of doubt, this page will look specifically at some of the best, proven, and popularly acquainted trading strategies with a high number of success stories.

Analysis

Ardent traders are always on the lookout for some of the best ways to maximize the cryptocurrency market. While this is no easy task, technical analysis of the crypto market can help you build formations that would fine-tune the way you pick up trends and ultimately trade your currencies. Technical Analysis may look scary and complicated, but the truth is that it is not.

Your ability to use technical analysis to make good trading decisions and make money in the cryptocurrency market is imperative. Suppose you do not understand the critical details in technical analysis, particularly studying patterns and charts. In that case, it could lead to aimless trading and unavoidable loss of money as a trader, or you would struggle to make profits over time.

In the crypto market, Technical Analysis can be referred to as historical price movements to make accurate decisions about the market. This means that there are steps taken in making accurate decisions regarding price movements in the market. Every part of technical analysis is based on price. Price trends are nothing more than higher highs and higher lows or lower lows and lower highs in price. Trends like structure, suppose, and resistance, and indicators are all formulas added to historical price data to plot that indicator on your charts.

Charts

Unlike the candlestick pattern, the chart pattern forms between ten to about fifty candles. They are identifiable patterns that can give traders an indication of possible reversals and market sentiment. They also point out possible entries in the market and help elevate your trading game. For most traders, chart patterns are easier ways to enter trades. Double tops and double bottoms are revered as the most proven chart patterns. In these patterns, there is a need for objective rules. Chart patterns indicate a market that sloops creates a level of support and then bounces up to a level of resistance.

Candlesticks Patterns

Candlestick patterns are candlesticks that form a specific way to help us determine what price is likely to do next. The shooting star candle, hammer pattern, engulfing pattern are lists of Candlestick patterns used by traders. Candlestick patterns can be used to help traders detect reversals and provide clarity on market sentiment. Additionally, these patterns can be used for entry reasons, trend continuation, and reversal trades. Candlestick patterns also form between one and a few candles.

Japanese Candlestick Charts

The core of any trading market is the candlestick chart. What a candlestick represents on a chart is the price movement throughout a certain period, depending on the time frame that you are on—the daily chart. For instance, if you are on a 5 min chart, each candlestick will represent five minutes of price movement.

Candlesticks are represented by two parts, which include the Body and the Wick. Using the time above frame, a green candle represents a five-minute period where the price of an asset went up or closed above where it opened. On the other hand, the red candle represents a five-minute period where the price closed below or went lower during the time frame.

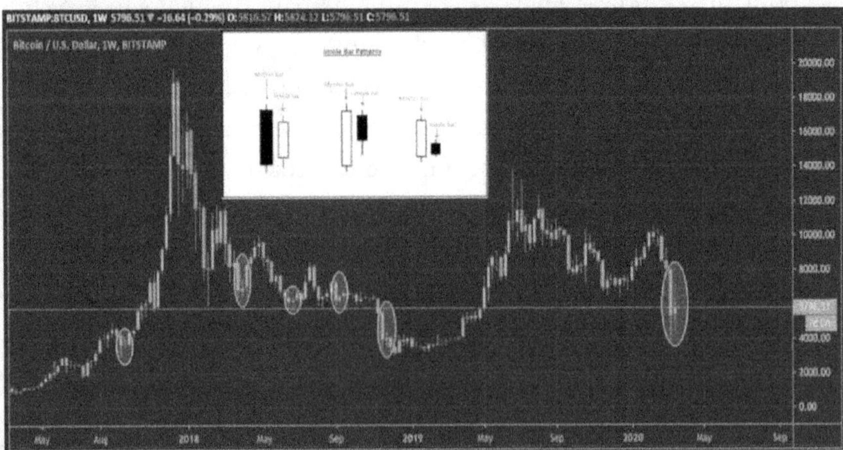

The opening of a green candle is where it opened during the time frame. For instance, if the candle's opening is at midnight, the candle will represent the open of a candle, while the low would be the lowest point the price got to during the specified time frame. Correspondingly, the high would be the highest point the asset's price got to during a five-minute window, and the close would occur at 12:05. This means that the current price at this time would be the ending price for five minutes.

For the red candle, we would have an opening at the top of the body due to the closing of price, or that time; it went lower during a five-minute window. The highest point on a red candle is the top or wick of the candle, which translates to the highest point price, got to within the time frame. On the flip side, the low is the lowest wick on the candle, while the close is the closing price after minutes of data on a five-minute chart (opening at noon and closing at 12:05). The candlestick shows you all of the action of price along with a specific time frame.

Indicators

Trading indicators are formulas added to the current and historical price and mathematical equations to plot lines and histograms on your chart. The purpose of trading indicators is to help simplify what price is doing. For instance, a candlestick chart can be very confusing, so trading indicators are meant to clean up some complexities. Indicators can also be used as an invaluable object rule in a trading strategy or in any form of trading to help create a more consistent trade. Essentially, trading indicators can help clarify market conditions, identify trends, areas of values, find entry points, and determine where you want to place your stops and targets. There are thousands of trading indicators in the cryptocurrency space, but the most proven and helpful indicator is the ATR Indicator. ATR stands for Average True Range. It is a strategy that gives you the average moment of price out of the last 14 candles. It works because it adds up the price movement in total—the total amount of pips. Each candle moved out of the last fourteen candles is divided by fourteen to give you the total average moment of price in the last fourteen candles. Note that any trading platform should have an ATR indicator. Traders often grieve the loss of money to trades, despite having an excellent reward to risk ratio. With the ATR Indicator, you can stay in line with the volatility of a market currency pair or time frame.

Trend Market

In the trend markets, there are significant aspects identified as the uptrend and downtrend. The uptrend is nothing more than when a candlestick chart consistently makes new highs and then higher lows. The reason for utilizing a trending market is because it gives your trade more accuracy, and as such, most traders gravitate towards the trend market. Trends markets can make up for better rewards to risk setups. It is an easier and safer bet to ride a trend that is already dominant than to pick the top or bottom of a market trying to trade reversals. In light of this, it is most preferable to trade with the trend.

To identify trends, it is best to take note of impulsive moves in a trending market. This refers to the big moves that break into new highs. After an impulsive move, the market takes a pause, which is regarded as pullbacks. The most objective way to identify these trends is that the lowest low of the pullback cannot be broken for a trader to stay uptrend. An uptrend market is considered high until you break the close below the lowest low of the past pullback.

Chapter 15. Relative Strength Index (RSI)

The Relative Strength Index is a trading indicator that illustrates whether an asset is overbought or oversold. It is a momentum oscillator that displays the rate at which price changes happen. This oscillator ranges between 0 and 100, and the data is usually displayed

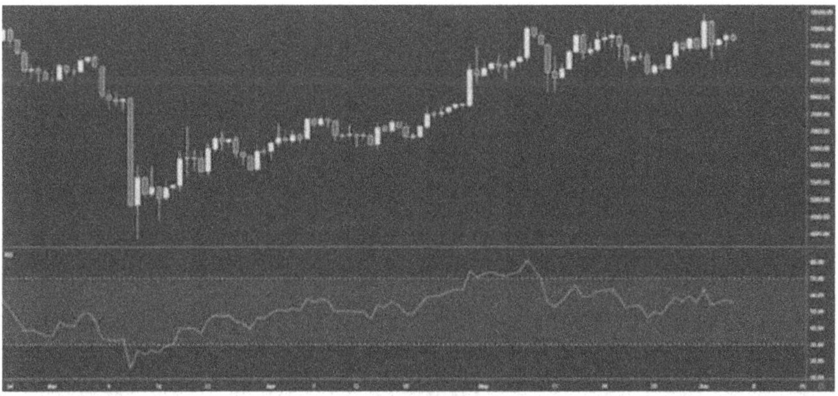

on a line chart.

What's the concept behind measuring market momentum? If the momentum is going up while the price is going up, the uptrend may be considered vital. If momentum is diminishing in an uptrend, the uptrend may be regarded as a weak one. In this condition, a reversal may become.

Let us demonstrate how the traditional interpretation of the RSI works. When the value of the RSI is under 30, the asset may be regarded as oversold. In contrast, it may be regarded as overbought when it's above 70.

Still, Relative strength index readings should be taken with a degree of skepticism. The RSI can reach very high values during noteworthy market trends—and even then, the market trend might continue for a while.

The RSI is one of the simplest technical indicators to understand, making it one of the best for new traders.

The Stochastic RSI (StochRSI)

The Stochastic RSI, also called the StochRSI, is a derivative of the RSI. Just like the RSI, it's the main goal to determine whether an asset is oversold or overbought. The RSI, however, the StochRSI is not gotten from the price data but RSI values. On most popular charting tools, the values of the StochRSI range between 0 and 1 (or 0 and 100).

The StochRSI appears to be the most useful when near the upper or lower extremes of its range. However, due to its higher speed and higher sensitivity, it may generate many false signals that can be difficult to interpret.

The usual way of interpreting the StochRSI is somewhat similar to that of the RSI. When it is over 0.8, the asset may be considered overbought. When it is below 0.2, the asset may be regarded as oversold. However, it's worth noting that these shouldn't be viewed as direct signals to enter or exit trades. While this information is sincerely telling a story, there may be other sides to the story. For this reason, most technical analysis tools are best used alongside other market analysis techniques.

Chapter 16. Supports and Resistances

We're going to look at a simple but effective idea of support and resistance regarding price charts. We will also look at how support and resistance can help us figure out turning points, entry points, and stop-loss points. Support and resistance are ignored or not given the weight they should be by plenty of new traders They're too preoccupied with Fibonacci levels, Bollinger Bands, MAC D-s, and Pivot Points to notice this crucial piece of market information. Because it is so crucial, we will first examine the principle of support and resistance. It comes naturally. It's where the market decides where things have become a little too expensive; or where things have become a little too cheap, and reacts accordingly. For example, if the price of oil fell to $45 last month and then rallied to reach $50, we want to see if the market sees value there again if it begins to fall back to $45 where it saw value a month ago. The expectation is that the buyers will return. But first, consider a hypothesis. We have a market that is falling, then rallies up to a level known as resistance level, where the market previously rallied, and it can't get through. Some might see a failure at resistance as an opportunity to sell short, with a stop above. Assume the market begins to fall again, as it did the last time. This can be done on a weekly, daily, hourly, or 10-minute basis. This concept of support and opposition can be found all over the place. The market falls; we may see a rally, but it does not break the previous low, indicating the possibility of support forming. Some people would see this as an opportunity to buy with a stop loss underneath the low. That's the theoretical version but plenty of people say, what if you could use just one indicator; would it be Bollinger Bands or Stochastics or MAC D? Well, it would be none of those. Instead, it would help if you should focus on support and resistance because it's the market telling us exactly where there is supply and demand and where there have been buyers and sellers.

Let's take a look at an example. This is a long-term example of

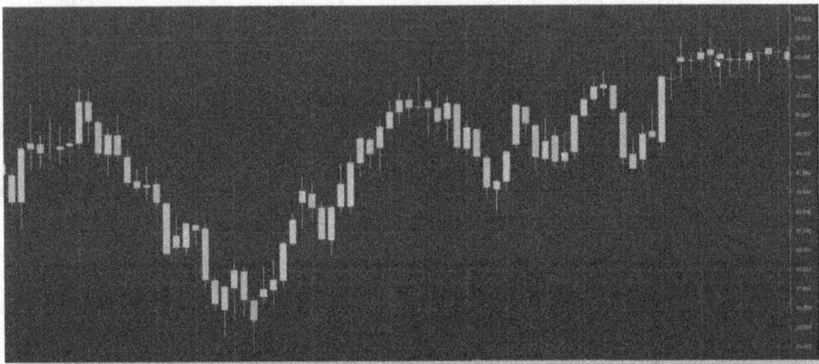

resistance. This is the price of oil.

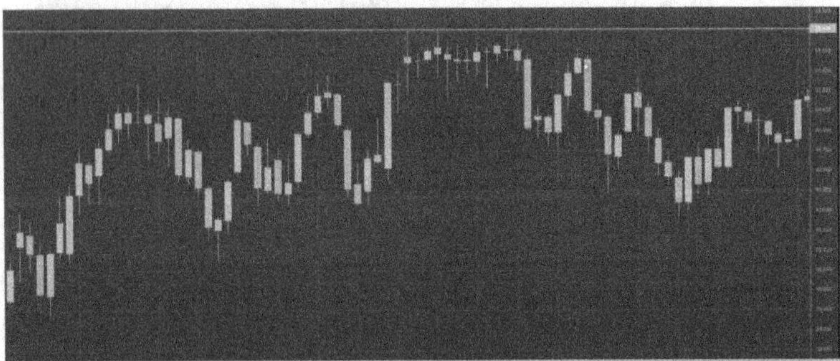

Each candle represents a week's worth of trading. What I'm interested in what was happening here. These are weekly candles. It's trying to break 55 dollars 20 cents and a few weeks later comes back to it again. About six weeks later, it's back to it again. So we have a definite level of resistance. Let's pick up on that. Let's move forward in time and see what happens next.

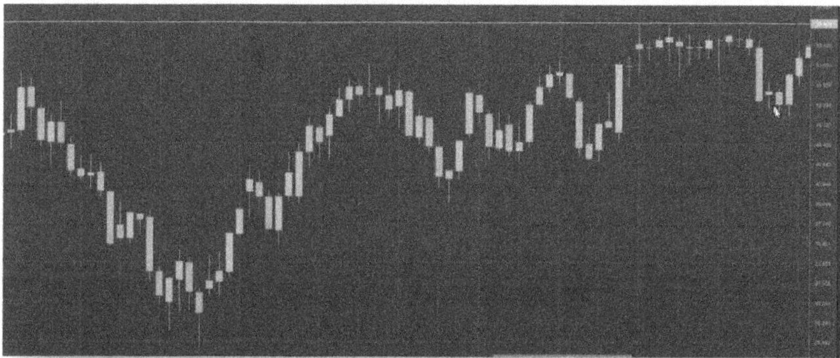

The market sells off below $48 then comes back for another go. That's resistance. People who think this resistance will stay in place might be looking to sell short with stops above, and if moving the timeframe again, you can see that would have worked.

The market did sell-off. It proved to be a high level at the beginning of the year and what's interesting as we head towards the end of the year is that we are back up here again.

So how is this resistance level going to perform an interesting one to watch?

The following chart is a slightly shorter-term example. What we're looking at is that we are having a look of support. It's a daily chart of the Euro Dollar. This is to the end of August, and it starts coming off, and we think where this market will stop? What we want to pick up on is past pull.

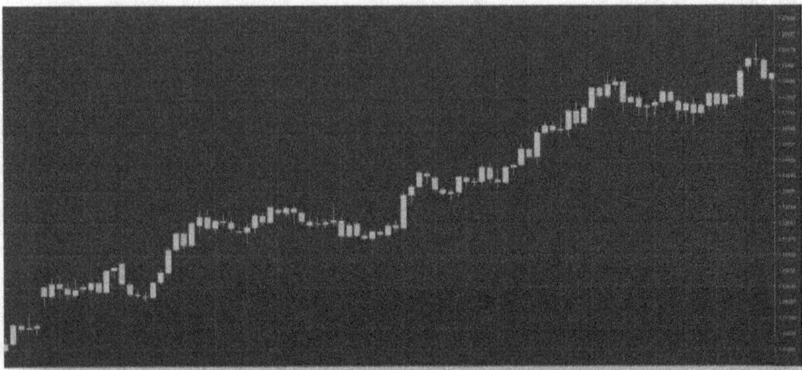

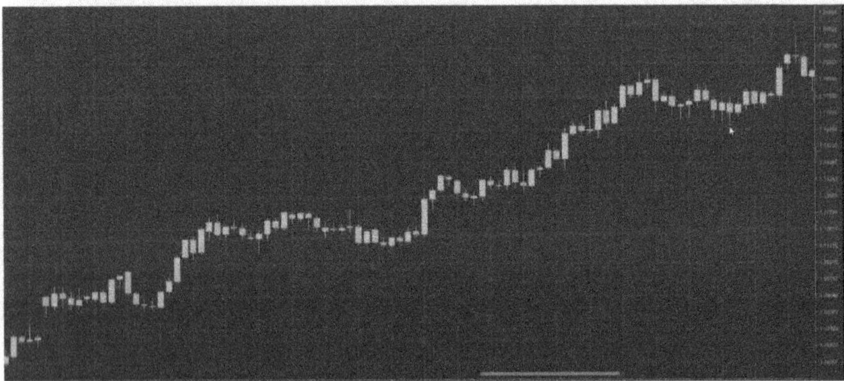

Here it's the dip down to towards 116,50 before the market rallied 400 points.

Let's pick that one up by picking up our horizontal line and putting it underneath those lows. So traders will be watching this level to see how the market performs. If it heads back down? Does it end up being support again? Because this market is so strong, that is what we'd expect.

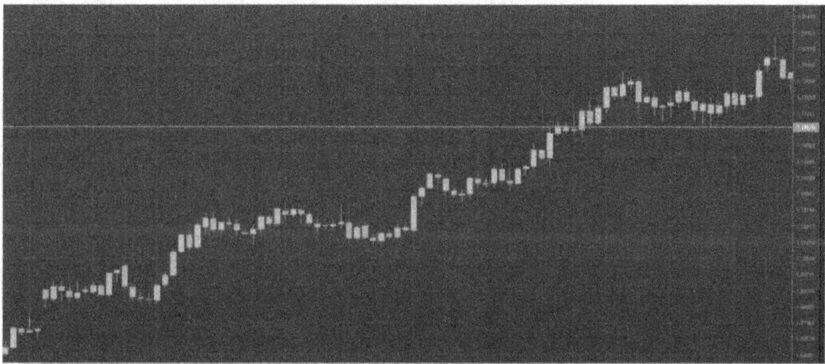

Let's jump forwards to October. The markets come off about 400 points. We're back down to the same level, and we see the slide stop. So a trade here would be to be a buyer with the stop-loss underneath that line.

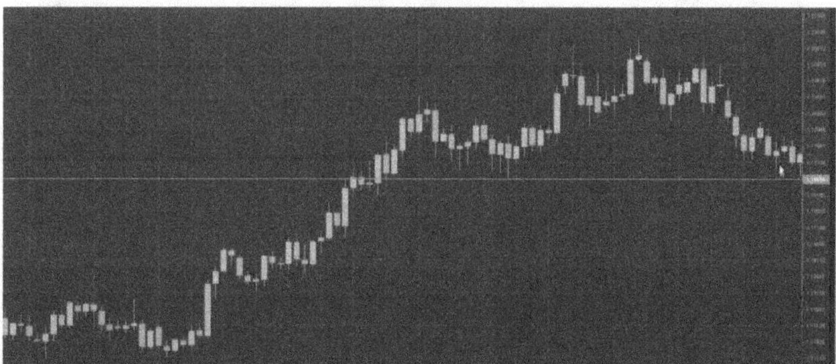

So let's jump forward a few more days. It's a short-term move, but the market does move higher. It moves a couple of hundred points off at that level so that support has done its job.

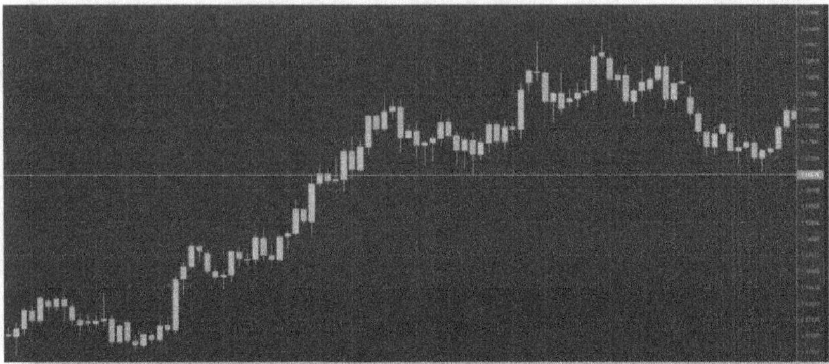

What's interesting now is what's happening with that support level. You can see the Euro is slipped below it. We've had one day where it slipped below, and we have seen some recovery.

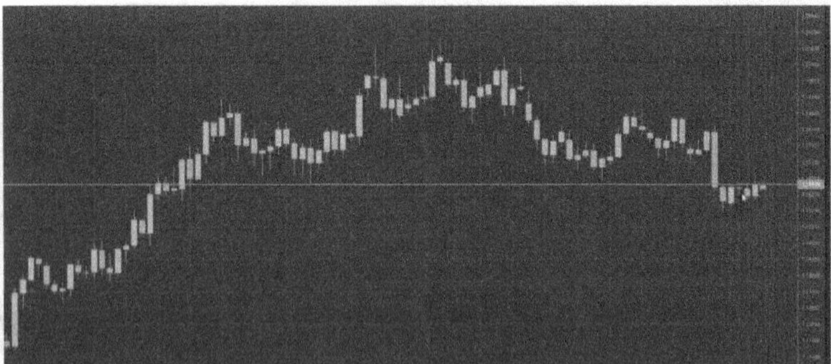

Hopefully, you can see how this support did prove to be a good entry point. For the final example, we're going to go much shorter term. We're looking at the US 30 market here. The Dow had been an incredible rally since the presidential election last year, but looking at this strength, we can pick up on past support levels. We were looking

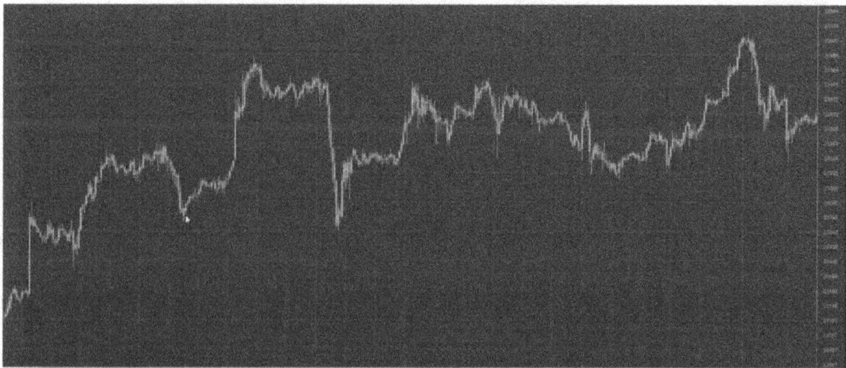

at the market here, and it ran from 23,270 as high as 23,490.

So it's a sizable rally. We might be thinking, where's the market going to stop. When it sells off? Well, we can pick up on the support. Admittedly, the market did spike below it by 10 or 12 points, but hopefully, you can see the principle here that these old levels can come back and prove to be high levels to trade-off.

This was back in October; a couple of days later, we see the market once again hold. When we walk this chart forward, if we see the market start to sell-off, we're looking at how it reacts by the support. Does it give us a good entry point? As you see, if you jump forwards, we can see a fair bit of volatility. The market sells off hard in the space of an hour and a half drops down about 120 points. But where do we see the buyers come back in? Well, we've got this chunk of support from 23000 through to about 20350.

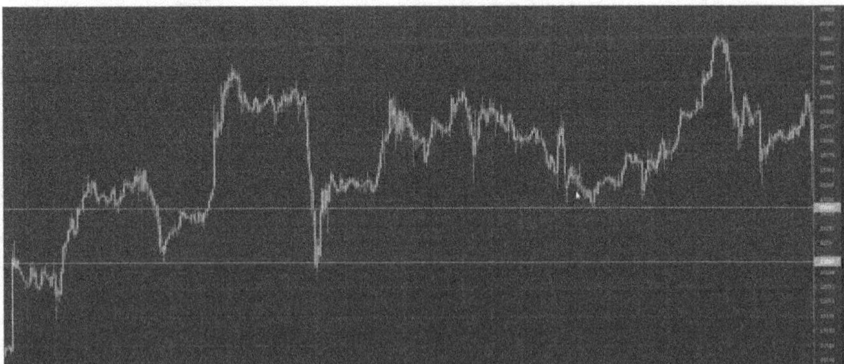

Once again, an aggressive trade here. We'll be buying into that support, and if we jump forward to where we are now, you can see that the market is bounced back and taking out these old past short-term resistance once again.

So it doesn't work perfectly, but it can give us a prominent area to initiate a trade and an area for a stop-loss point, and an area where if things have changed, we can see on the chart. We've looked there some simple entry points. If you don't look at support and resistance

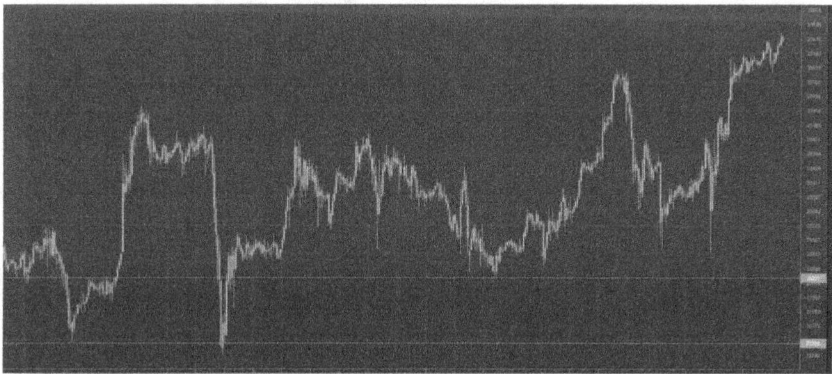

yet, you should start looking at it regarding where you want to place your trades and place your stop losses.

Chapter 17. Price History

2011

Bitcoin price started at $0.30 per BTC and grew to $31.50 by June. Commercial transactions with bitcoin had started with Silk Road accepting it as payment.

2012

Started at $5.27 and grew to $13.30. The Bitcoin Foundation started in September 2012 to promote the development and encourage its use.

2013

Started at $13.30 and experienced price fluctuations from $775 to $1163 before falling to $760 by the end of the year due to blockchain forks that arose. The seizure of bitcoin from Silk Road and Mt. Gox, as well as the blind auction of the seized assets to Tom Draper, affected prices this year. Another significant impact on the bitcoin market is the cryptocurrency ban China placed on its financial institutions.

2014

The price kept started at $770 and closed at $314 by the end of the year, during which the Wikimedia Foundation started accepting bitcoin donations. The FinCEN also implemented regulatory guidelines for the bitcoin miners. A significant event in 2014 that affected the price of bitcoin is the split in the blockchain into two independent chains operating on different versions simultaneously.

2015-2017

Prices rose from $315 to $998 by the beginning of 2017.

2017-2019

Prices rose from $998 at the beginning of 2017 to $13412.44 by the beginning of 2018 and then fell to $6914 by February 2018 due to the ban on crypto trading by China. It closed at $3747 by the end of 2018, and by June 2019, the price of bitcoin was $13000.

2020-present

2020 ushered in the pandemic, and the price fell below $4000 in March 2020. It witnessed a comeback after the $250 million MicroStrategy investment in the market, and by November 2020, the price hit an all-time high of $19860. In 2021, prices hit $37299 after a tweet from Elon Mush with a #Bitcoin, and prices have continued to rise since then. Prices presently are above the $50,000 mark.

Storing Bitcoins

As a digital currency, bitcoin cannot be stashed in banks or underground, and it is stored electronically. Sue to the growing number of hackers and thieves has become essential to keep the bitcoins safe to avoid losing them. It is also possible to lose bitcoin due to loss of the access keys, computer failure, crashed hard drives, loss of computer, etc. And once bitcoin is lost, it cannot be gotten back. However, there are several ways of keeping bitcoins safe from potential loss. Bitcoins are stored in a digital wallet which could be hardware or software. Storing bitcoin in wallets also ensures verification of transactions and gives easy access to the bitcoins as well.

Chapter 18. Understanding Price and Volatility

If you're going to invest in Bitcoin or any cryptocurrency for that matter, it's essential to understand the market factors that drive the price one way or another. Many of these often interact with one another, but we will examine them one by one for simplicity purposes.

China

No country has a greater influence on Bitcoin's price than China. China has more fiat to Bitcoin trades than any other country, and it is home to some of the world's largest exchanges. The Chinese market accounts for roughly 70% of all Bitcoin trades worldwide.

Good news from China is good news for the market as a whole. The People's Bank of China's December 2013 announcement that Bitcoin was not a currency crashed the market by 35% in less than an hour. In contrast, news of Bitcoin adoption by Chinese businesses frequently causes the Bitcoin price to rise.

The Chinese government's strict financial regulation of assets held in the Chinese Yuan is one of the major factors driving the Bitcoin market. Both wealthy and middle-class Chinese citizens are looking for a way to secure their financial future without being reliant on the Yuan's recent depreciation. Bitcoin is the ideal method for them to accomplish this. Furthermore, Yuan depreciation will only lead to future Bitcoin growth.

Russia

Russia, like China, is having problems with its fiat currency, the ruble. For the past three years, the ruble has been falling year on year against the US dollar. Russians prefer to protect their wealth by converting their rubles to Bitcoin.

Bitcoin's short-term price movements are also influenced by adoption in Russia. The market reached an all-time high of $1800 in May 2017 after Ulmart, Russia's largest online retailer, announced that it would begin accepting Bitcoin payments.

Government Regulation

The price of Bitcoin as a commodity will be influenced by government support. Although Bitcoin is not linked to any one country, it does require government support to gain widespread adoption. The perceived "complete anonymity" of Bitcoin and its link to crime, particularly tax evasion, are the main points of contention for governments right now. Government support and the price of Bitcoin will rise once measures to eliminate the anonymity element are in place (regardless of your moral position on this).

On the other hand, whenever there is news of a government crackdown on Bitcoin, whether as a digital currency or as a technology, the price drops.

Technological Innovation

If Bitcoin is to maintain its value, advancements in the network are required. As previously stated, new developments such as SegWit and the lighting network will alleviate scalability issues and are critical in the technological development of the coin.

One important factor that influences future value is the coin's ability to handle micropayments (small monetary transactions). The 1MB block size currently limits the system's effectiveness for micropayments, resulting in minimum transaction amounts and payment processing delays if you send too many transactions too quickly. The team hopes to alleviate these issues and increase Bitcoin's real-world viability by implementing the lightning network.

Mass Media

Despite popular belief, the vast majority of people still get their news from only one or two sources. To put it bluntly, the mainstream media has no idea what Bitcoin is all about. Due to a lack of suitable cryptocurrency or crypto-asset journalists working for major outlets, they would instead air good soundbites like "Bitcoin could reach $100,000 within five years" or "Bitcoin is the biggest bubble since the dotcom craze," then examine it on a technological level or focus on any innovations that have been made, rather than examine it at a technological level or focus on any innovations that have been made. Positive media coverage of Bitcoin attracts new investors, while negative coverage results in a price drop.

On the other hand, some Bitcoin commentators have already formed opinions without even examining the technology. You can safely disregard any news item from 2017 that mentions Bitcoin as a front for "drug dealing" or "money laundering."

I recommend dedicated sites like http://coindesk for legitimate, non-biased, or overhyped news about Bitcoin and cryptocurrency as your news source.

Funding for Blockchain Companies

As blockchain companies continue to receive more funding and investment, the currency receives more legitimization. Many blockchain-related startups now accept investments in Bitcoin and other cryptocurrencies like Ethereum.

The Middle-Class Investor

A frequently overlooked factor. While Bitcoin is gaining traction among younger investors and some larger institutions, it remains largely unknown to the American middle class. To put it another way, consider Tom, a 55-year-old Marylander. He's married, and his upper management job pays him a low six-figure salary. His current holdings are primarily blue-chip stocks and low-cost index funds. He isn't attempting to hit any home runs; rather, he is attempting to protect his retirement assets. Bitcoin's value will continue to rise once it establishes itself as a form of "digital gold" that is more of a long-term investment than the speculative toy it is viewed as by some major institutions. In other words, we need more people like Tom as our target Bitcoin buyer for the value to continue increasing.

Technical Analysis

Because the cryptocurrency market is a) only eight years old, it lacks comprehensive data, and b) unlike anything we've ever seen before, traditional technical analysis or chart analysis like one would do on stocks is difficult. Charting, on the other hand, has a place in the Bitcoin universe. If you want to trade Bitcoin on a deeper level, I recommend studying stock technical analysis books, with candlestick charting being the most useful for the cryptocurrency market.

Mass Adoption

The more merchants who accept Bitcoin as payment, the more legitimate the currency becomes. The primary determinant will be Bitcoin's scalability issues. The rate of adoption is increasing, and the total number of businesses accepting the currency is increasing. If major corporations like Amazon and Apple start accepting Bitcoin payments, the price will rise once more.

Chapter 19. Strategies and Tips

Options Trading

So what exactly are the options? Well, their name says a lot of it. They confer on a holder the right but not the obligation to buy or sell an asset at some time in the future. When you enter a "call" option, it's the right to buy, and when you enter a "put," it is the right to sell. They differ from futures instruments in that futures must buy or sell the asset that you've entered a trade for. Basically, with an option, if you find that exercising the right to buy or sell is not profitable on expiry, you can let it expire worthless. With a future, you have to either cash settle it or buy/sell it. This means that options are instruments with asymmetric payoffs.

There's also another side of this option crypto coin. You can also sell options. This, of course, limits upside and could lead to unlimited losses. Why would anyone sell these, you ask? Well, they can form some pretty unique trading strategies with them, something that is covered in a bit.

When it comes to options, several variables or inputs impact their value. These are the strike price, the spot price, the time to maturity, the underlying implied Bitcoin volatility, and the risk-free rate. The strike price is the price at which you agree to buy or sell the option in the future. The spot price is the price right now. Time to maturity is how long the option has to go, and implied volatility is a measure of how risky the market is. Each of these factors impacts the value of the option in its unique way. The difference between the strike and the spot has perhaps the most direct impact on value. However, holding other factors equal, the higher the volatility, the more valuable. The longer the times and maturity, the more valuable. These variables or inputs are often labeled the Greeks. They are called the Delta, Gamma, Vega, Theta, and Rho. The exact mechanics and maths behind these inputs can be pretty complicated. There is one more thing that I briefly need to discuss, and that is the "moneyness" of an option. The relationship between the spot and the strike price has the most significant impact on the option's value.

Simply put, an option could be in the money, at the money, or out of the money. Here is what they mean. The money is when the spot is above the strike for a call option or if the spot is below the strike for a put option. Out of the money is when the spot is below the strike for a call option and vice-versa for a put. At the money means the strike equals the spot price.

1. So let's take a look at some options that are about to expire soon. We're looking to determine how much speculative buying or selling pressure is likely to come in the spot market from the expiry from these calls or puts in the options market. Basically, to get a rough back of the envelope put-call ratio. Next, you can further the range of options to those relatively close to the money level. Here you might choose an acceptable range for both. In my opinion, Bitcoin will most likely be trading within the 21K to 23.5K range on December 21st. As a result, I examine all of the options that fall within this range. On the call and put sides, I'd like to calculate the total outstanding notional or open interest. The total open interest on the calls is around 4200 Bitcoin as of these option expirations. The total notional outstanding on the put side is around 1770 Bitcoin. So, as we get closer to the December 21st expiration date, we can see that there are nearly 2.4 times as many cool positions in the market. So theoretically, this means that there is more chance of there being buying pressure in the spot market as we head into the expiry than selling pressure. A more bullishly positioned market. Of course, I should caveat that there were

still about two weeks to expiry when doing this analysis. A lot can change closer to the expiry date, and as I mentioned before, in the Bitcoin markets, the impact on spot markets of the open expiry only tends to be felt two or three days before. So, if you're going to be using this analysis method, I would encourage you to re-examine the relative open interest balance as we get closer to the expiry time.

Margin Trading

People believe that natural decentralized alternatives do not exist, or that if they do, they require a Ph.D. to operate. That is, until dYdX made their protocol public. Everything you need to know about dYdX will be revealed to you. I'll also walk you through how to use dYdX to trade lending and borrowing, as well as compare it to other apps. So, what is dYdX exactly? Simply put, a non-custodial decentralized crypto exchange, or DEX, is what it is. Unlike most other Dexes, however, you can borrow, lend, and trade on margin here. It's a smart contract-based open-source trading protocol based on the Ethereum protocol. Given that it's non-custodial, it means that no one else but you are in control of your private keys. Trading is done by connecting your Ethereum wallets to the exchange. No KYC, no limits, no questions.

Let's look at some of these features, starting with their primary MO; margin trading. Trading on the margin means increasing the size of your exposure to an asset through leverage. At the large centralized exchanges such as BitMEX, the exchanges will loan you a position in underlying crypto for only a small deposit, the margin. With a leverage position, your gains and losses are magnified by the leverage factor. At a decentralized exchange, they will monitor your positions, and if they deteriorate to a certain level, you will be liquidated. This is all done by the internal liquidation engine that these exchanges run. You can't see how these engines work, and you don't know all the parameters used in those algorithms. At dYdX, on the other hand, the protocol is open-source. Fully auditable smart contracts adjust leverage ratios, free up margin and, if need be, liquidate positions. You can see exactly how the protocol works in a fully transparent manner. Leverage at dYdX goes up to a maximum of five times or an equivalent margin position of 20%.

Options Expiry Dates

I want to touch on the option expiry dates, specifically the impact that this tends to have on the spot market. If you follow any crypto news website or trading group, you'll sometimes hear references to the "option expiry dates." If many options are expiring on the date, this could indicate that there's likely to be quite a lot of volatility on the day. So the critical question here is; why and how can you judge the likely price direction on the expiry date? Let's start with that first one. There is volatility around these expiry dates because market participants try to adjust their positions to deliver the underlying asset's physical delivery.

As the option price approaches these pivotal moments, some market makers may need to adjust their hedge positions in the spot market. As a result, you have a situation where option expiration events have a direct impact on the underlying spot markets. The impact on the spot market is likely to be greater when there are a large number of outstanding options. This has been known in the equity markets for a number of years. These are the so-called expiry weeks, when the underlying share's volatility begins to rise. However, as Bitcoin options have grown in popularity, we've seen these instruments have an impact on the Bitcoin spot price. This usually happens about two days before the expiration date. On the expiration date, those who hold the option may either close out their position or roll forward into new options. So, when it comes to price movements, we know that option expiry dates are usually dates of interest. Is there any way to predict which way it'll go? Well, there's no hard and fast rule, but you can get a general idea by digging deeper into the order books' options.

Step-by-Step Checklist for a Trader Plan

One of the biggest mistakes that you can make is not having a clear trading plan. Without a plan, you're trading blind. To help you always have a trading plan from now on, I'm going to present you with a step-by-step checklist that walks you through every aspect to consider before sending any trade order. If you go through all these steps, you should never again be in a trade that you don't know what to do with. Let's now go through this trading plan template. First of all, I recommend taking a look at upcoming events. Even though this doesn't directly affect your trade, looking at future events before opening a trade can save you from unwelcome surprises. Are there any upcoming dividend payments earnings or other upcoming events that might clash with your trade plan? Around these events, stocks often behave differently, and they usually would. So, either be aware of this or avoid trading through these events. Next, define your risk. Never open the trade without knowing your max loss. Way too many traders don't do this even though this is a must to manage the risk. Besides defining your risk, you should also define your reward. Have a clear profit target that tells you when to take profits. Without a clear profit target, it's easy to tell yourself to wait for just a little more. Doing this will lead to winning trades turning into losing ones. After defining your max risk and Max reward is straightforward to calculate your risk to reward ratio. So make sure to do precisely that. Calculating and seeing your risk-reward ratio will give you more insight into the payoff of your trade. A good rule of thumb is that your risk to reward ratio is better than 1 to 2, but note that you should also take the probability of profit into account. It's ok that your risk is more significant than your reward as long as your probability of profit is high enough.

Furthermore, it would help if you should also define the time frame of your trade.

Chapter 20. Advanced Strategies

When you are looking forward to capitalizing on the small frequent price movements, day trading strategies are the best for you. Any effective strategy you will choose must be consistent and must rely on in-depth technical analysis that utilizes charts, market patterns, and price indicators predicting future price movements.

It is your responsibility to choose the most appropriate strategy that best fits your requirements. As a trader, it is good that you know the average daily trading volume.

Fallen Angel

A Fallen Angel is a strategy that involves a bond that has been reduced to junk bond status from an investment-grade rating due to the issuer's weakening financial conditions. In terms of stock, a fallen angel refers to a stock that has always been high and now has fallen considerably. Fallen angel bonds can be a sovereign, corporate, or municipal debt that a rating service has downgraded. The main reason for such downgrades could be attributed to revenue decline that generally jeopardizes the capabilities of issuers to servicing debt. The potential for downgrade often experiences a dramatic increase when expanding debts are combined with expanding debt levels. The securities of fallen angels are at times so attractive, particularly to contrarian investors who seek to capitalize on the potential. This enables the issuer to recover from the temporary setback.

Example:

Due to the ever-falling oil prices over several quarters, an oil company has reported sustained losses. The company, therefore, can decide to downgrade its investment-grade bonds to junk status as a result of the increasing risk of default. This will result in a decline in the prices of the company's bonds and increase yields, which will make the contrarian investors attracted to the debt as they only see the low oil prices as a temporary condition. However, there are conditions where you are likely to go at a loss, significantly when the fallen angel bond issuers do not recover. For example, if there is an introduction of superior products by a rival company, the issuers may fail to recover.

ABCD Pattern/Reverse ABCD Pattern

The ABCD pattern is a pattern that shows perfect harmony between price and time. ABCD pattern usually reflects the standard and rhythmic style in the market movements. The geometric price/time pattern consists of three consecutive price trends with a leading indicator that can guide a trader to determine when and where to enter and exit a trade. As a trader, ABCD Pattern can be essential in identifying the available trading opportunities in any market (be it futures, forex, or stock) on any timeframe (be its position, intraday, or swing) and in any market condition (be it range-bound, bullish or bearish markets). Before placing a trade, ABCD Pattern can help you determine the reward and the risks of trade.

Bull Flag and Bear Flag

With technical analysis, a flag refers to a price pattern that can explode and move within a shorter timeframe to the prevailing price trend that has always been observed in more extended time frames on a price chart. With the flag patterns, a trader can identify the possible prevailing trend from a given point where the price has drifted against the same trend. Therefore, if the trend resumes, by noticing the flag pattern, there will be a rapid price increase, which makes the timing of a trade advantageous. Flags are areas of tight consolidation in price actions, and they show a counter-trend sharp directional movement in price. This pattern has 5 to 20 price bars.

Bullish Flag Formation

These are formation patterns observed in stocks that have a strong uptrend. Bull flags got their names from the fact that the pattern closely resembles a flag on a pole. A vertical rise in stock results in a pole, and a period of consolidation results in a flag. The flag is usually angled down away from the prevailing trend and can be a horizontal rectangle. The bullish flag pattern starts with a substantial price spike that is almost vertical. The prices then peaks and form an orderly pullback where the lows and the highs become almost parallel, making them almost form a tilted rectangle.

Bearish Flag

Comparing to the bullish flag, this flag is an upside-down version of the bull flag. The bearish flag is an inverted version of the bull flag. In this case, an almost vertical panic price drop is formed by the flagpole because the sellers make the bulls get blindsided, and, as a result, there is a bounce having parallel lower and upper trend lines, forming the flag. The panic sellers are triggered when the lower trend lines break. This flag is similar to the bull flag in that the severity of the drop on the flagpole will determine how the strength of the bear flag can be.

Develop Trading Skills

To become a trader, you are required to not only know about just finance or business but also hard science or mathematics. You must be an individual who can do deep research and analysis that can mirror the economic factors from a broader perspective and the day-to-day chart patterns impacting different financial markets. As a trader, it is crucial that you need to sharpen your ability to concentrate and focus, especially in a fast-moving environment containing different people with different goals and ideas. You must also be able to practice self-control and regulate your emotions even when in situations upsetting you. Lastly, you should always keep an accurate record of your trades to check on your account and provide you with a learning opportunity to help you become a better trader.

Chapter 21. Pros and Cons

Pros

Exchanges are a very convenient way to buy and sell cryptocurrency, and once you understand how they work, they can also be an effective way for you to make money in the long term.

Convenience

The most significant advantage of using an exchange is convenience. Exchanges have made it very easy for people to buy and sell cryptocurrency, and you do not need any special knowledge or experience to get started.

You will need a cryptocurrency wallet to store your coins, but you do not need to worry about any complicated software or hardware. All you need is an internet connection and a few minutes of your time, and you can start buying and selling coins right away.

Liquidity

Another advantage of using an exchange is that they tend to be very liquid. This means that there are usually plenty of buyers and sellers available on the platform at all times, so you can easily find someone who wants to buy or sell the coin that you want. Many people use this liquidity to increase their profits in the long term by buying low and selling high on exchanges.

Accessibility

Exchanges are also straightforward to access. You do not need any special permission from the government to start using them, and you can start trading almost immediately after opening an account. It is also relatively easy for new users who have accounts with banks or payment providers like PayPal or Skrill to deposit their funds into their accounts.

Low Fees

Exchanges also have some of the lowest fees in the industry, which means that you will profit even when you pay a commission on your trades. Most exchanges charge between 0.25% and 0.5% in commission fees each time you make a trade, but this is still much lower than the fees charged by most investment platforms and brokerages.

Security

Exchanges generally have extreme security measures in place, which means that your coins will be safe while they are stored on the platform. However, it is still important to store your coins in a secure wallet that is not connected to any centralized exchange. You should also make sure that you do not share your private keys with anyone else.

Ability to Buy Altcoins

Exchanges have made it very easy for people to start buying altcoins. Most of the exchanges that allow you to buy Bitcoin automatically allow you to buy other altcoins as well. All you need to do is sign up for an account and deposit some coins into your trading account, and you will be able to start trading instantly.

Transaction Speed

Most exchanges have breakneck transaction speeds. In most cases, you can start a trade and have it completed in less than a minute. This is not always the case, and it may take longer for certain coins to be transferred from your wallet to your trading account. However, this is still a much faster process than making a bank transfer or sending a wire transfer through an online payment provider like PayPal or Skrill.

Wide Selection of Coins and Trading Pairs

Exchanges are by far the best place to find a wide selection of coins and trading pairs. This is because most exchanges list every single coin available on the market today and add new ones regularly.

Cons

Despite all of the advantages that exchanges have to offer, they are still far from perfect. In this part, we will be looking at some of the most significant disadvantages of using an exchange and how you can avoid them.

Exchange Fees

One obvious disadvantage of using an exchange is that they all charge fees for their services. The commission fees on exchanges usually range between 0.25% and 0.5%, but this can still seriously eat into your profits over time if you are not careful.

You will also need to pay fees for every trade you make, and these fees can vary from one exchange to the next. Some exchanges also charge a flat fee for each transaction, which can be as high as USD 20 and can seriously eat into your profits.

Security Risks

Another major disadvantage of using an exchange is that they are not as secure as other brokerages and investment platforms. Even though many exchanges have extreme security measures, this does not mean they are perfectly secure. The coins that you buy on an exchange are stored in "hot wallets" instead of cold storage, which means that they are more vulnerable to hackers and other security threats than cold storage coins.

To fully protect yourself from security risks, you will need to transfer your coins from their hot wallets into a secure wallet that is not connected to the exchange itself. You should also use an offline wallet like a hardware wallet or a paper wallet rather than a software wallet on your computer or mobile device.

Lack of Transparency

Another disadvantage of using an exchange is that they are not very transparent. Most exchanges do not even disclose the names of the people who own them, which means that you will have no idea who is running them or their business practices. The only way to be sure about an exchange's standards and practices is to read from other users and do your research.

Government Interference

Although most cryptocurrencies are designed to be free from government interference, some countries are still a possibility. For example, China has recently banned all ICOs and local cryptocurrency exchanges in the country, which has hurt trading volumes and prices across the board. If this type of thing happens in other countries, it could severely impact your profits in the long term.

Lack of Support for Fiat Currencies

Many exchanges have stopped accepting fiat currency deposits over the past few years. This means that you will need to purchase an alternative cryptocurrency like Bitcoin or Ether and convert it into the coins you want instead of depositing your cash directly.

There are some exceptions to this, such as Coinbase that accepts fiat currency for those in the US, but it is not an option on most exchanges. As a result, you will need to buy an alternative cryptocurrency from an exchange that offers this service and then convert it into the coins you want at another exchange.

Chapter 22. Mistakes to Avoid

For most, trading can be challenging, regardless of their experience level. The trading strategy, emotions, and analysis all play an essential role when it comes to doing your best.

However, more often than not, a trader will end up making some mistake. No matter your experience level, the following are the five most common mistakes made by traders.

Tops and Bottoms: The interest in grabbing a bottom or top is tempting. There is a significant appeal in a contrarian market approach, but unless there is an excellent reason, lock in your profits before the top of a top or bottom of a bottom.

The main reason why a trader will chase the tops and bottoms is psychology. Traders think that the market, especially right after a strong trend, will change to enter a new trend. This can lead a trader to take the wrong position. The fact is that trends can only be validated when the price has moved considerably from its support or resistance level, and even the best traders or analysts will find it extremely hard to call a bottom or top. To ensure you do not fall prey to chasing tops and bottoms, you have to set your impulses and emotions aside and look at the market objectively.

Trying to pick a top or bottom is common, but it has an equally significant risk. Traders should turn to other strategies like Bolinger Bands, high-low methods, or divergence. This helps predict when the momentum will be exhausted.

Bad Risk Management: The exciting thing is that, for the most part, traders tend to be correct in their analysis. What they tend to get wrong is their money management. Entering a prominent position quickly because your analysis shows that the prices will probably turn may end up leaving you at risk of the prices continuing to grow.

When you have too much first position exposure, it may become difficult to manage your trade goes wrong. There are two golden rules that every trader should follow.

1. Always expect your first position to be wrong and use a minor first position.

2. Increase your position when your first position is proven to be correct.

These two rules will enable you to think critically, lower your losses and increase profits. Please read these rules every month to ensure they are set into your trading plan.

Allowing Losses to Pile Up: One of the essential characteristics of a successful trader is getting out of a position with a slight loss quickly if they see a trade is not going to work out, and they then move onto the next trade. On the other hand, the unsuccessful trader will become paralyzed if their trade goes against them. Instead of acting quickly to cap their loss, they tend to hold their position in the hopes of the trade working out. In addition to tying up their capital for an extended period and becoming a bag holder, this type of inaction could cause mounting losses and depletion of their capital.

Failure to Make Use of Stop-Loss Orders: This is a mistake linked to the one above. To be successful in trading, you have to have use stop-loss orders. The failure to implement this one is the worst mistake that you can make. A tight stop-loss typically means that a loss will be capped before they become too large. A 10% stop-loss below your buy price is usually sensible. So if you invest $100, you can only lose a maximum of $10, returning the majority of your capital.

Not Sticking to or Not Creating a Trading Plan: Experienced traders always need to have a trading plan. The plan will help traders know when they will enter and exit, how much they will invest, and the max loss they will take. A novice trader may end up not having a plan before they start trading. Even if they have a plan, they are more likely to abandon it than the more experienced traders if they think things will not plan.

Avoiding the above mistakes can preserve your capital and mitigate your risk when entering into the world of Cryptocurrency trading. Cryptocurrency is a highly volatile asset and can deplete your funds quickly if the correct measure is not taken. Conversely, if they are implemented with a good trading plan, the rewards are immense.

Chapter 23. Manipulation Tactics and How to Avoid Them

Cloud mining allows ordinary investors not to need expensive cryptocurrency mining equipment. After the success and rapid demand for bitcoins worldwide, the number of new cryptocurrencies is growing. Bitcoin has not left the site since the launch of the dispute. It has resulted in hundreds of wealth stories, but it has also allowed fraudsters to make millions of dollars on unsuspecting buyers and investors.

The price of bitcoin fluctuated around $ 9,000 for several days, making it a profitable investment opportunity. The biggest challenge facing the bitcoin industry worldwide is regulation. While bitcoin can become part of the general portfolio of ordinary people, there is still a long way to go. Ashish Agarwal, the founder of Bitbuddy (startup of the bitcoin market), said: "Governments themselves have great difficulty managing bitcoins, but they can regulate exchanges and other crypto service providers. Mobile application first gets to know the company and its founders. Be prepared for them, check their recognition."

Mr. Agarwal added: "Never get into mining schemes; there is no such thing as a real business. There are more than 5,000 identified cryptocurrencies in the world. 99% of them are a scam. Everyone thinks bitcoin is expensive; invest in some cheap coins. "Please don't just look at the price; look at the maximum offer, the turnover offer, the market capitalization, the trading volume for the last 24 hours, the most crucial concept, and the team behind the coin. Always be careful who you are and what you invest in. If you want to invest in bitcoin, here are the essential precautions to keep in mind.

Fake Crypto Investment Platform

Fake bitcoin exchanges—a real threat! Back in 2017, the fake Korean exchange operated under the name BitKRK. Although it seemed legitimate and presented itself as part of the cryptocurrency community, it misled millions of dollars before investors and buyers stopped the Korean financial authorities. It would help if you avoided all fake cryptocurrency exchanges. Follow only reputable and recognized bitcoin exchanges. Browse the Bitcoin forums and subscribe to actual RSS feeds or notifications to receive timely news about fake exchanges. Or stick to reliable bitcoin platforms for a real investment opportunity.

Other Less Reliable Cryptocurrencies

After the success and rapid demand for bitcoins, several new cryptocurrencies are growing around the world. It is tough to trace the authenticity and effectiveness of each of them. New altcoins can be cheaper, making them a profitable investment opportunity for most new investors. The idea of selling these new currencies is that it is too late to invest in bitcoins, and you need to take the opportunity to invest in one of the new and future coins to make more money!

Well, that's not entirely true. Keep in mind that My Big Coin was withdrawn after selling counterfeit alternative currencies for $6 million to customers. However, it is essential to consider the basics of any altcoin, including its maximum supply and turnover. For example, the maximum supply of bitcoins is precisely 21 million and 18 million in circulation. Bitcoin is one of the most valuable, reliable, and accepted cryptocurrencies in the world.

Mining Scam

Cloud mining allows ordinary investors not to need expensive equipment for cryptocurrency mining. This can be beneficial considering that you can mine altcoins, such as bitcoins, at home without investing in overpriced equipment. Some cloud mining services allow users to rent fixed-rate server space for altcoin mining. However, if you invest for the first time, how do you know which services are genuine and which services want your earned money?

One way to identify counterfeits is through their high promises. They promise a great return on your investment and never mention the hidden fees that apply to that return. These servers are cleverly designed to get money from unsuspecting investors. No honest company can guarantee a profit. Be careful when registering on a cloud mining server. Think about the security of the data on your system before you go online on a shared server.

Pump and Dump Fraud

It is not uncommon for fraudulent groups to buy new altcoin in bulk. This momentarily raises the cryptocurrency market price and causes FOMO (fear of missing out) among other investors. As soon as new investors start investing in the new currency and the price rises, fraudsters will sell their coin shares at a higher price.

This is illegal in the stock market, but pumping and resetting are more common than in the gray area of cryptocurrency. Avoid pumping and dumping schemes by choosing more popular and stable cryptocurrency options, such as bitcoin only.

Malicious Software

New investors are not always familiar with cryptocurrencies before and during investing. This created an opportunity for the development of many malicious programs. Malware now poses new and more significant threats to everyone. Modern malware targets cryptocurrency users and investors can hack users "accounts to retrieve balances in users" wallets online, withdraw their accounts, and replace their accounts. In addition to updating your antivirus program and system firewall, you need to ensure that you are on a secure and reliable platform that does not require you to download .exe files or ask you to download them automatically.

Chapter 24. How to Avoid Crypto Scams

The number of scams currently infesting the space is one of the reasons why crypto can be so intimidating for newcomers. Some are quite obvious, while others are more subtle and almost convincing. Scammers must adapt in order to stay profitable, so they've been able to con users who thought they were immune. Is one of these con games just around the corner for you? This page serves as a comprehensive guide to crypto scams, as well as a top five list of those to avoid. I'll also share some helpful hints for avoiding scams, hacks, and other dirty tricks. The Ponzi scheme is the first and perhaps most well-known scam I'd like to discuss. This is older than cryptography, which dates from the 1920s. It was named after Charles Ponzi, an Italian fraudster who used the Ponzi scheme to defraud investors. A Ponzi scheme's basic premise is straightforward. Typically, an operator will pay out existing investors with funds raised from new investors. The company does not generate any legitimate revenue. It gives the appearance of income, which may persuade many of those who have invested that it is legitimate. This will continue as long as new investors are available to provide capital. These schemes frequently ask users to refer others. It's for this reason that it's sometimes called a pyramid scheme. Although the fundamentals of a Ponzi scheme are fairly simple, some of them can be difficult to spot.

Some Ponzi schemes can go on for years and deceive even the most seasoned investors. Bernie Madoff, for example, ran one of the most long-running and deceptive Ponzi schemes ever. His victims were sophisticated hedge funds, mutual funds, and high-net-worth individuals, not your average retail investor. Everyone agreed that Bernie's services were in high demand. There are waiting lists for his investments. Look at all the other wealthy people who believe in

Bernie. In the crypto world, there have been numerous such schemes. An exit scam is generally easier to set up than a fiat Ponzi scheme. They also adopt a variety of guises or fake business operations to justify their profits. To avoid raising too many questions, they frequently choose methods that appear to be credible. I won't go over all of the examples, but here are some of the most well-known Ponzi scheme front businesses. Platforms for crypto lending With these, you'll provide capital to a platform, and they'll pay you interest on a regular basis. Borrowers are on the other side of the equation, paying interest, according to the MO. On the surface, it appears to be a viable business model. The devil, however, can sometimes be found in the details. If this is a centralized lending service with annualized interest rates that seem completely out of whack, it should set your alarm bells off.

For example, during the Bitconnect era, they paid out monthly interest rates of over 40%. This seemed absurd and unsustainable, especially for such a mysterious project. We all know what happened to Bitconnect, of course. Cloud mining is another common crypto Ponzi scheme. The scheme will claim that your money is being mined for cryptocurrency and earning a steady return. Of course, the money you put in does not go toward mining equipment and instead helps to keep the scheme going. There have been a few of these in the past, but the Bit Club network is perhaps the most well-known. They lasted for more than five years and raised more than 720 million dollars from investors. Many people suspected them of being a Ponzi scheme, but it was difficult to prove that they were not investing the money in mining equipment at the time. Of course, the FBI had access to personal communications and was ultimately responsible for sinking that ship. Some investment schemes are another well-known crypto Ponzi scheme. They'll either claim to trade cryptocurrency or have a trading bot that can generate consistent profits. These are the kind of Ponzi schemes that are pretty easy to avoid. The truth is that any service that claims to have a fantastic trading strategy or trading bot does not require your funds. They might be able to profit from their trading strategies. It's all a ruse to get money from you in order to pay out previous investors. There have been a number of these in the crypto world as well. Amfeix is one of the most recent examples. By the middle of 2020, they had brought in nearly $60 million.

That was until they used the money in an exit scam. How do you avoid crypto Ponzi schemes now that you have a basic understanding of how they work? The first and most important red flag to look for is if a scheme promises you a specific amount of profit. Nothing is guaranteed, and statements like these should set your alarm bells ringing. I know what you're thinking: your pal claims to have a consistent source of income month after month, and he most likely did. This is how a Ponzi scheme operates. To persuade the investor that they do work and, as a result, want to invest more money, the investor may choose to refer our friends and family. And while we're on the subject, this is usually another Ponzi red flag. You should avoid a scheme that offers you bonuses and perks for referring others and tiers those referral levels. This is multilevel marketing at its most shady. This has been used in nearly every crypto Ponzi scheme in the past. High-profile promoters would be at the top of the pyramid, making money off those below them. Don't be fooled by platform advertisements or publicity. Bitconnect was promoted on Coindesk, Coin Market Cap, and a number of other websites. Billboards were also removed. Ponzi schemes, like any other type of project, are ad buyers. Because they require new victims, they are likely to spend more on advertisements than legitimate businesses.

Advertising platforms, media sites, and influencers don't always take the time to research the product they're promoting. A Ponzi scheme is similar to an empty drum. Empty drums produce the most noise. The infamous giveaway scam is our next scam, which is also quite common. Simply put, the scammer is attempting to persuade you to send them money in exchange for your money being multiplied. Send us one Bitcoin and we'll send you ten in return. Despite how ridiculous that may sound, these con games are quite effective. They usually portray the promotion as a prize giveaway by a project influencer or a celebrity of some sort. They promote these scams through popular social media platforms. Most of the time, this is through impersonation, although they do sometimes manage to hack accounts. For example, you'll undoubtedly have seen that high-profile Twitter hack in 2020 where scammers managed to get into the accounts of Joe Biden, Elon Musk, Kim Kardashian, etc.

They were able to make almost $150,000 by Tweeting the giveaway scam, and if you think that's a lot of money, consider what some of the earlier iterations of these scams were able to generate. Scammers were making over a million dollars in a string of these giveaway promotions before Twitter cracked down on bot manipulation tactics. My personal favorites were the ones created by Elon Musk. They were sometimes so convincing that they fooled major news organizations. However, as Twitter has cracked down on these scams, they have become less common. Scammers, on the other hand, have found fertile ground on YouTube. You've probably seen live stream giveaways where users are encouraged to participate by watching an interview. Users are directed to a website with instructions on how to send money and how their money will be multiplied. These have proven to be quite successful, and they've recently begun using YouTube ads to distribute these videos. Recently, it appears that YouTube has cracked down on some of these con artists. They may, however, appear in unexpected places, so you must be able to recognize and report them. They'll try to disguise the message in some way. Fake transaction evidence and time-sensitive pressure tactics may be used. They will try to appeal to our emotional love for easy gains and quick promotions, but you must take a step back and ask yourself, "Is it reasonable for someone to offer me free money on the internet?"

That is a question I'm sure we all know the answer to. A phishing scam is the next scam I need to warn you about. This is yet another attack vector that can be employed in a variety of ways. The goal of a phishing scam is to trick you into giving up sensitive information so that a hacker can access your cryptocurrency. Phishing scams aren't limited to cryptocurrency; they've been used to gain access to people's online bank accounts, email accounts, and other password-protected accounts. A typical crypto phishing scheme involves convincing you to visit a website that appears to be legitimate. They could be in a password-protected exchange, an online wallet, or some other service. Scammers will usually try to use a domain address that appears to be very similar to the site's official address. They'll either rearrange letters, add a hash, change the spelling, or use a different domain extension, such as dot net or dot-info. The truly cunning will go so far as to replace a letter with a number. A ledger with a l or a ledger with the l replaced with a capital I for example. It's quite convincing. Homograph attacks will be used by the most sophisticated hackers. Unicode characters from non-Latin writing systems like Cyrillic or Greek are used in these. They can make a domain look exactly like the one intended. These domains usually host sites that look very similar to the one you're considering visiting. Most likely, this is a login panel for the service in question. You think you're logging into your account, but you're actually giving the scammer your personal information. They can access your accounts and, of course, do whatever they want with your coins once they have your login information.

Chapter 25. Types of Crypto Investors

There are several types of cryptocurrency investors, each with its methodologies and investment strategies. This post will identify these different types of investors and their strategies for maximizing returns.

Type 1: HODLers seek long-term gains by holding onto assets rather than selling them for fiat currency such as the US dollar in anticipation that the asset will increase in value over time.

Type 2: Day traders make trades throughout the day based on short-term price changes. These traders use technical analysis to guide their trades.

Day traders often use the same strategies used by technical traders, and only they do it faster and more frequently.

Day traders look to profit from short-term price movements in altcoins by buying up altcoins that they think are undervalued and then reselling them immediately after they have been purchased for a higher price. This is a risky strategy because the market can be highly volatile.

Day traders look to trade altcoins created by significant projects with the excellent marketing potential to generate short-term gains. For example, if they can sell a coin that has been promoted through a well-known social media outlet at a discount, they can make some money. Altcoin day traders make money by selling coins that are well-known in the community and for which there is a demand.

Day traders are also most likely to consider fundamental analysis when they make trades. They will look at the coins with robust code but may not be well-known in the community and are therefore undervalued.

Type 3: Wannabe investors use the internet to shop around for the best possible investment. This is not an investment strategy that will generate significant returns, but it can hedge against losses should a cryptocurrency be canceled or fail in its original function.

Wannabe investors do all they can to avoid making a significant investment in cryptocurrency by looking for the following most popular altcoin that is the next big thing and investing heavily in it.

Wannabe investors view cryptocurrency as a get-rich-quick scheme and are more interested in individual coins rather than the entire market as a whole. This strategy is high risk and does not have a lot of potentials to make consistent gains.

Type 4: Technical traders seek to find underlying support and resistance levels in the market based on historical movements with hopes of capitalizing on the next significant move up or down.

Technical traders are the most likely to take losses if their coin is canceled or fails in its original function. If a cryptocurrency is no longer needed, why would anyone still use it?

Technical traders make trades based on the signals and information that they receive from other technical traders.

Technical traders may also focus on specific coins based on real-time information regarding the markets as a whole. For example, if there's a vast altcoin dump in IRC channels, many technical traders will likely try to buy as much of that particular coin as they can before the dump occurs.

Type 5: Arbitrageurs profit from the price difference between two exchanges by buying low and selling high at other exchanges.

Arbitrageurs look for significant price movements between exchanges that are out of sync with one another and then buy on the cheap in hopes that they can sell it at the same time it's being bought at other exchanges at a premium. This is a risky strategy to follow, as there is no telling how long it will take for prices to return to normal.

Type 6: Investors who use fundamentals-based trading look to identify undervalued assets and invest in them in the hopes of generating gains.

Investors who use fundamentals-based trading are typically just looking to generate profits through long-term investments. They are not seeking the next breakout altcoin that is going to go big overnight. Instead, they are looking for coins with actual use cases and clear development goals.

Type 7: Altcoin traders seek to capitalize on the popularity of a certain altcoin in hopes that it will increase in value. The cryptocurrency market is highly volatile, so it's not uncommon for traders to make money off short-term price movements.

Altcoin arbitrageurs profit from the crypto-to-crypto price difference between exchanges or between two places where it is possible to exchange crypto for fiat currency. Trading altcoins for one another is an excellent way to generate a quick buck. Still, for those who are not familiar with how cryptocurrencies work, it can be challenging to use this strategy effectively.

Type 8: Long-term investors use fundamental analysis based on investment strategies to maximize returns over long periods. These strategies are typically built around strong teams, clear development goals, and real-life use cases for the blockchain technology on which the coin is built.

Long-term investors invest in a coin because they want to understand the underlying technology and develop it further. As long as the underlying technology remains strong, these investors will likely continue to hold onto coins bought at low prices during their early days.

Long-term investors focus on fundamental analysis of altcoins rather than technical analysis of individual coins. This strategy focuses on utilizing the code behind each coin to predict its future development and long-term potential.

Type 9: Short-term investors are seeking short-term profits to be made using short-term price movements. These investors typically hold their assets for a few weeks or months before selling them in hopes of generating a quick profit. This strategy does not yield many great returns to start with, so it's natural that many people would hodl instead.

Short-term investors use sites like Reddit and Twitter to be alerted to which altcoins are performing well at any given time. These investors may even place a limit buy order on specific altcoins before it hits the market so that they can buy large amounts when it's cheap, then sell them off before they shoot up in value. They may also short sell altcoins that they think will crash.

Short-term investors may also use fundamental analysis based on investment strategies designed to generate gains in altcoins, but they have a different outlook than long-term investors. These investors tend to look for coins with the potential to yield short-term gains before they sell them off for fiat currency.

Chapter 26. Investor Guide

Remove Your Ego

Losses are mainly encountered when investors take pride in their enormous profits.

When you profit with a proven and tested working investment strategy, you can pride yourself on the accumulated success.

But profits made with no investment plan or strategy will one day lead you to lose not only your profits including your total investment.

When price moves unexpectedly, it doesn't necessarily mean losses. Instead, it happens because investors made wrong trading.

Learn to Live with Losses

No one likes losses, but everyone enjoys profit. When a price drops below your entry can lead to loss; when a position is liquidated at your entry can also lead to loss.

As an investor living with losses is part of the investment, so fashion your mind towards that.

Hopes and Prayers Does Not Guarantee Your Success

Most traders mistake taking a small profit and let the losses run, hoping the price will return to their entry point.

The reason for an investment plan is to have access to your average performance; it helps you keep your profits and losses in check by putting your stop loss and consider profit and calculating your risk to reward ratio before opening your position.

Hoping in trading is gambling, some will decide to wait for a bit of bit, praying and hoping to make a profit on their loss; yes, it may have worked for you before, but it is not the ideal way of trading; it could blow up your investment in the long run.

Know Yourself

This is one of the difficulties encountered by beginners; I could remember my trading experience as a beginner when anxiety gets hold of me, especially if I am at a loss, I keep sweating profusely.

In trading, do not invest money that will affect your psychological well-being; remove the orientation of making millions of dollars in a short period so you won't get disappointed.

I often enter a trade with a loss mindset, so I do not feel disappointed if I lose eventually. Anyway, that's what works for me, so you need to look out for your strategy.

Do not Double Your Losses

Most times, we open uncalculated or planned entry positions in the quest to recover from losses which will, in turn, double the losses when the market price goes persistently against our entry.

Know Your Limit or Pain Level

This mainly occurs when investors change the strategy without tangible reasons or because they found a new strategy.

There is no perfect trading strategy or concept. Each strategy has its advantages and disadvantages. I will advise you to choose a strategy that suits your limit or one you can absorb or endure the pain level.

Be Disciplined

Many traders failed because they lack this attribute in them.

Controlling your emotions and using your strategy at any point in time guides you to calculate your mistakes and improve on your investment.

I could remember opening multiple trades because I was not disciplined at first and could not overcome my emotions, resulting in blowing up my investment capital.

Be Comfortable with Your Strategy

Most successful traders are contempt with their trading strategy; no matter what the market does, they stick to that strategy that works for them.

No strategy is 100% percent accurate, but when the profit you make is more significant than your losses after your accumulations, the strategy is functional, but if not, try and improve on the strategy.

Have a Trading Plan

If you fail to plan, you plan to fail. Many successful traders have a unique trading concept for opening their entry points whenever they get a signal.

Do you know that your investment capital determines the amount of trade to open? How many times do you intend to trade in a day or a week? These are things you have to put in your plans for successful trading.

Earning from Trading Is Not Easy

I am not trying to discourage you, but I must tell you the truth: making money from trading Forex, stocks, commodities, bond, and cryptocurrency is not easy. You have to position your psychology to work on the rules guiding trade.

There are still some lucky ones who make a quick profit on investing in the Forex market and another financial chart trading, but I am looking at the number of people it favored.

Diversifying Your Risk

Despite how promising a product might seem to be, I would always suggest you risk it with a good systematic approach.

Many traders have basic knowledge or information of the product and trade them profitably daily but remember their information might not be disposable to the public, so I always encourage people not to risk all their investment in one product no matter how promising the product may sound.

Chapter 27. Trading Psychology

Gambler's Fallacy

The gambler's fallacy is incorrectly over or understating the likelihood of an event based on a series of past events. This can be illustrated with a simple example of a coin flip. The probability that a coin will land on heads is 50%. No matter how often you flip a coin, this probability does not change. So even if your coin just landed on heads ten times in a row, this does not affect the probability of the following coin flip. As the name implies, the gambler's fallacy is widespread in gambling. But this pattern of thinking is quite common in trading as well. Let me give you some examples. Have you ever opened a long position because the stock had many consecutive down days or vice versa? If so, you have fallen prey to the gambler's fallacy. Another example would be the reaction to losing or winning streak. If you ever felt that after many consecutive wins, the chances of losing increased and you decreased your position size, you have been guilty of the gambler's fallacy.

The Law of Small Numbers

You've probably heard of the law of large numbers, which states that the average of a growing sample size converges to the population's actual mean. This is a well-known probability rule that allows you to estimate the parameters of a population using large enough samples. However, as the name suggests, this only works with large sample sizes. This is where the law of small numbers fallacy comes into play. The law of large numbers is commonly misapplied by most people, specifically with two small sample sizes. Let me give you an illustration. Have you ever tried a trading strategy for a handful of trades and then concluded that it doesn't work? If so, you have been guilty of using the law of small numbers. A few traits is not a big enough sample size to give you any critical information about the quality of a trading strategy.

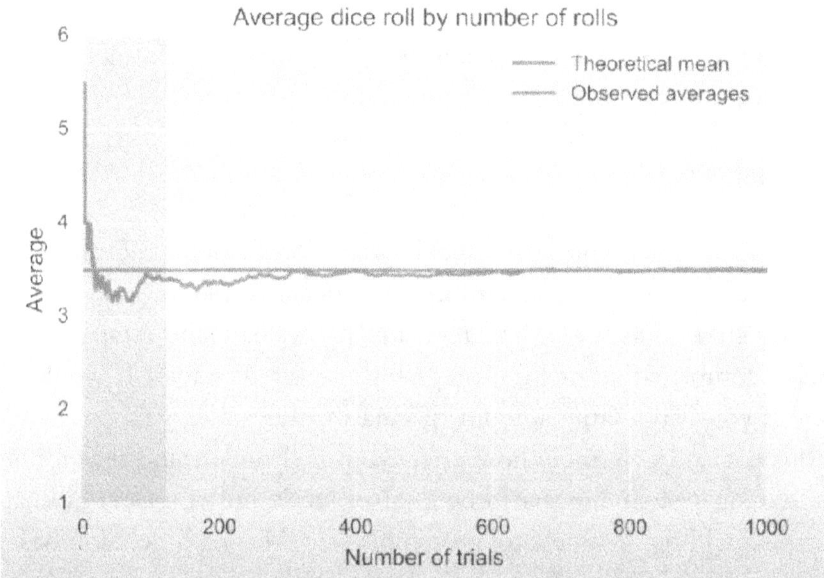

How can the law of small numbers be avoided? You must, after all, thoroughly test the effectiveness of a trading system. The goal is to make at least 20 trades with this trading system. It can be intimidating to use a new trading system for more than 20 trades when you have no idea how well it will perform. As a result, you should reduce your risk to a level where you can afford to lose on all 20 trades. The goal of these trades is to test the trading strategy rather than make money. Try to be as mechanical as possible when making these 20 trades. Create clear rules for every market scenario imaginable and follow these rules on every trade. If you don't have a clear set of rules to follow, you can't reliably test your strategy since there is no strategy to test.

Additionally, track entry prices, exit prices, profit potential, money at risk, time in the trade, and more in a detailed and thorough trade journal after each trade. You're ready to evaluate the strategy after you've completed all of these steps for at least 20 trades. It would be ideal if you had a large amount of data on this strategy so you could evaluate it and determine how effective it is. I understand that testing the trading system appears to be a lot of work, but you can't evaluate anything without a large enough sample size. Making a decision based on a single or two events is equivalent to claiming that roulette has a 100% win rate because you won one round.

Correlation

Additionally, track entry prices, exit prices, profit potential, money at risk, time in the trade, and more in a detailed and thorough trade journal after each trade. You're ready to evaluate the strategy after you've completed all of these steps for at least 20 trades. It would be ideal if you had a large amount of data on this strategy so you could evaluate it and determine how effective it is. I understand that testing the trading system appears to be a lot of work, but you can't evaluate anything without a large enough sample size. Making a decision based on a single or two events is equivalent to claiming that roulette has a 100% win rate because you won one round. Is it true that if asset A and asset B are highly correlated, a change in the price of A causes a reaction in the price of B or the other way around? Another causation bias is failing to consider that the third variable could be the cause of two correlated variables. Two oil stocks, for example, may be highly correlated, but that doesn't mean that a move in one causes a move in the other. Instead, a third factor, namely the oil price, could be to blame for the stock's movements.

Finally, two variables can be correlated without having any causal relationship. You're almost certain to find some variables that are correlated solely by chance if you have a large enough set of data. The correlation between per capita chicken consumption and US crude oil imports is an example of such a coincidental correlation. Over the last ten years, these two variables have had a nearly 90 percent historical correlation.

Nonetheless, I wouldn't use chicken consumption data to forecast crude oil imports into the United States. There are numerous other examples of seemingly illogical connections. As a result, never assume that correlation equals causation in the future. It's easy to prove correlation, but proving causality is a different story.

Confirmation Bias

The tendency to seek out information that confirms your pre-existing beliefs is known as confirmation bias. Without a doubt, the vast majority of traders have been guilty of this bias. It's only natural to seek out information that confirms your trading idea after you've opened a trade. You could examine dozens of indicators or social media posts and only pay attention to those that support your beliefs. Finding something that you agree with is a great feeling, and it can help you feel more confident in your positionThis causes you to miss signs that your trade isn't the best idea and that something is wrong. Instead, you continue to convince yourself that everything is fine. If you search Twitter for a ticker symbol, you're almost certain to find at least a few people who believe the same thing about the market. However, this is meaningless. Having a clear set of indicators and rules to follow for your trades is one way to avoid confirmation bias in trading. If you have such a clear set of rules and indicators, there is no need for you to go out and look for any other confirming signs. Furthermore, it is best to avoid social media as a trade decision-making guide.

Winners and Losers

Most people believe that putting in more effort yields better results. Most jobs, for example, are compensated per hour, but this isn't always the case in trading. It doesn't mean you'll make money just because you spend countless hours studying an asset's fundamentals, technicals, or anything else. You could even lose money and a trade that you worked on for a long time. Trading is a high-stress activity. It's difficult to watch your hard-earned cash vanish before your eyes. However, large gains have an emotional impact. Trading puts us in a constant state of uncertainty. You could lose money in a single day, but you could also make money. It's not uncommon for people to lose weeks or even months of profits due to a single bad trade.

Nonetheless, emotional trading must be avoided at all costs. Allowing emotions to influence your trading decisions can have a significant negative impact on your trading performance. When your hard-earned money is on the line, it can be difficult to keep your emotions in check.

The Right Mindset

The proper mindset is prevalent among traders. Too many traders judge the quality of their trades solely on the basis of their results. This is an extremely flawed method of assessing your trades. A trade with a 70% chance of making $200 and a 30% chance of losing $100 is unquestionably fantastic. Even if it succeeds, three out of ten times, this trade will fail. That doesn't make it a bad deal, though. Unfortunately, many traders use this method to evaluate their trades. Technical analysis appears to be so appealing due to hindsight bias. Finding chart patterns on historical charts is simple, but without the benefit of hindsight, things are much more difficult. If you've ever felt like a previous price move was so obvious, you've fallen victim to hindsight bias buyers. To avoid hindsight bias, you must evaluate your trades in some way other than by their outcome. Instead, focusing on the quality of your decisions along the way would be beneficial. Did you have a clear trade strategy and plan? Did you follow it if you did? If not, why not, and how could you improve your performance next time? In general, having a consistent way of evaluating your trades that is unaffected by the outcome of your trades is preferable.

Chapter 28. Discipline

I will explain how you can develop a winning attitude in trading. But first of all, why psychology and trading are even important. Well, trading is a unique activity. It's unlike every other activity that you can imagine. In some cases even contradict some beliefs that we have acquired throughout our lives. Let me give an example of this. Most people think that the more work you put into something, the better results you will get. For instance, most jobs are paid on a per-hour basis, but this isn't necessarily the case for trading. Just because you spend countless hours analyzing the fundamentals, the technicals, or anything else of an asset doesn't mean that you will make money. You may very well even lose money and a trade that you spend countless hours preparing. Trading is a very emotionally demanding activity. Seeing your hard-earned money vanish in front of your eyes isn't easy. But also, huge gains do affect your emotions. Trading confronts us with constant uncertainty. May very well lose money on a day, but you may also very well make money. It's not uncommon to see people lose weeks or even months of gains on one bad trade.

Nevertheless, it is important to try to avoid emotional trading. Letting emotions influence your trading decisions can dramatically decrease your trading performance. It can be tough to control your emotions when hard-earned money is on the line. Five fundamental truths can help traders to develop a winning mindset. First of all, anything can happen. In essence, the markets aren't anything else than millions of different people expressing their thoughts about different assets. People that think in assets prices low will likely buy, those that think in assets prices high will sell, and others will wait for a better opportunity. But every single trader of these millions of people can impact the price. Therefore theoretically, anything is possible. But even though everything is possible, not everything is likely. The probability that an asset's price will rise by hundreds of percent is relatively slim. However, the probability is not zero. It is possible. This brings us to the second fundamental truth. You don't need to know what is going to happen next to make money. You don't only don't need to know what is going to happen next. You can't know what is going to happen next. We just learned that the markets aren't anything else than millions of people expressing their beliefs. If you know what's going to happen next, you would have to be familiar with the beliefs of all of these millions of people interacting with the markets. It's safe to say that this is impossible, but that doesn't matter. You can still make money in the markets. If you have the trading system with the true edge, it does not matter what will happen next?

Well, the outcome of the next trade is irrelevant. For example, a casino has a true edge. The odds are on their side. Let's take roulette as an example. The casino has a higher probability of making than losing money on a game of roulette. However, they do not know what will happen on the next roulette spin, nor do they care. They may very well lose money on the next spin of a roulette. But that doesn't matter to them because they know that they will win in the long run. The same goes for your trading. As long as you have a trading system with the real edge, all you have to do is stick to that trading system. The outcome of your next one-two, or even more trades, does not matter. As long as you stick to your plan, the numbers will work themselves out in the long run. The next fundamental truth is that there's a random distribution between wins and losses for any given set of variables that define an edge. This goes hand-in-hand with the past truth. Just because the odds are in your favor does not mean that you will be right. Let's look at our casino example once again. The odds of winning a game of roulette are strongly in favor of the casino. However, that does not mean that they will win guaranteed. They will still lose money on some games. If you believe in a random distribution between wins and losses, could you ever feel betrayed by the market?

If you flip the coin and guess right, you wouldn't necessarily expect to be right on the next flip simply because you were right on the last. Nor would you expect to be wrong on the next flip if you were wrong on the last flip. Let's move on to the next fundamental truth. An edge is nothing more than an indication of a higher probability of one thing happening over another. Hopefully, this is relatively simple by now. Once again, I'd used the casino example to explain this. In a game of roulette, the casino has a higher probability of making than losing money. So that is their edge. The final fundamental truth is that every moment in the market is unique. If this weren't the case, it would mean that every single person and entity that interacted with the market during a past moment would have to do the same thing again. They would all have to enter and exit their positions just like last time. This is more or less impossible, and therefore every moment in the market is unique. If a moment isn't unique, you would have to know every variable, which once again isn't possible. So what are the takeaways of these five fundamental truths? Well, first of all, you do need a concrete trading system with definite rules.

Otherwise, you wouldn't have an edge, and then trading would be pointless. Remember, random trading will lead to unexpected results. Besides a trading system, you also need a trading plan. It would help if you always created a trading plan before every trade. It would help if you created your trading plan before opening a trade because that's the only moment you still can think 100% rationally. After you enter a trade, your hard-earned money is at risk, and then your emotions will influence your decision-making. Some key components of your trading plan should be your max risk, your max reward, your risk to reward ratio, your exit point, your entry point, your adjustment point, your position size, and ideally even more. If you truly believe in the five fundamental truths, you will automatically create a trading plan before every trade. For instance, if you believed that you don't know what will happen next and anything is possible, you would always define your risk and cut your loss. If you believe in your edge and all the truth, why would you do it from your trading plan? Why would you revenge trade or double up to make back the losses from a past trade? Why would you ever feel emotional pain if you believed in your edge? Does a casino feel emotional pain just because it lost on a single game of roulette? No, and neither should you.

The more specific your trading plan is, the better. If you have trouble sticking to your trading plan, write it down. In theory, your trading plan should be so concrete that you would be able to give it to someone else who could execute the entire plan without asking you. The more specific a trading plan is, the less you will have to think about what you're going to do, and thus, you will trade more mechanically. Another tip for trading more mechanically is using trade alerts. If you know that they're going to exit or adjust a position if a price reaches a certain point, you can set an alert at that point. As soon as that price is reached, you will get notified and adjust your position without thinking about it. Alternatively, you could use automated orders like stop losses or take profit orders. But probably one of the most important takeaways is that you should trade small. You should never risk more than a few percent of your total capital on one trade. If you truly accept the risk before entering a trade and keep your position sizing small, you will never have trouble sleeping at night. Remember that you don't and can't know what's going to happen next, and therefore, it's not unlikely that your next trade will be a loser. If you risk all of your capsules at once and the next trade will be a loser, you will lose all of your capital at once.

That's a disaster that you should never risk. This is also why casinos said betting limits. They know that they can very well lose on a single game of roulette. If someone wants to bet millions of dollars on a single game of roulette, the casino will likely decline. Because it knows that the odds aren't heavily in its favor. Their edge only really works in the long run when the number of occurrences is high enough. It would help if you thought the same way with your trading. So never risk too much of your capital at once. If you're currently familiar with the seemingly profitable trading system but somehow can't manage to be consistently profitable with it, it might be due to your mindset. So instead of trying to learn tons of new trading strategies, you could try to focus more on your psychology.

Chapter 29. Best Tax Softwares

A significant issue exists. Crypto taxes are complicated, and most accountants will flee if the word Bitcoin is mentioned. It's all too easy to bury your head in the sand and forget about those heinous games. However, those gains must eventually be accounted for. I'll go over a few options for crypto tax software.

CryptoTrader.Tax

It does this by allowing crypto traders and investors to quickly calculate their capital gains, losses, and taxes due. Although this option is primarily targeted at the US market, international support and taxes can be calculated for any country that accepts the FIFO and LIFO standards. All of these calculations can be done in almost any fiat currency. What features does the crypto trader tax have? It does, however, include an easy-to-use tax file. This is how it functions. You need to create an account to import those crypto transactions from your exchange accounts using the API import tool, or you can alternatively upload the trade history CSV file.

After you've imported all of your trades, you'll need to add the source of your cryptocurrency income to the current tax year. The good news is that this tax platform can calculate profits from a variety of crypto-specific sources. Mining, forks, airdrops, staking, and even gifts are all possible. Finally, you'll be prompted to choose your preferred tax calculation method and the tax form you'd like to generate. The tax report generated by CryptoTrader.Tax will include a variety of documents, including an income report, the 8949 IRS form, an audit trail report, and a short and long-term sales report. You will also get an end-of-year positions report and a TurboTax online direct import file.

That means you can import that report into other conventional tax tools like Turbo Tax or Tax act. Another appealing feature of CryptoTrader. Their tax-loss harvesting feature is called tax. That means you'll be notified about cryptocurrencies that offer a good tax-saving opportunity, which will help you plan your taxes better in the long run. The tax platform also allows accountants to import tax reports on behalf of those who want their report reviewed by a qualified accountant before submitting it to the government. If you want things double-checked for you, this is a great tool.

So, how much will this tax software cost you? The hobbyist plan, on the other hand, costs $49 per tax season. This includes up to 100 trade imports, free report previews, live chat support, unlimited revisions, IRS forms, cross-platform integration with tax filing software like TurboTax, tax-loss harvesting, FIFO, and LIFO computing, as well as tax-loss harvesting, FIFO, and LIFO computing. For $99 a year, the day trader plan includes all of this as well as support for up to 1,500 transactions. The high-volume trader plan unlocks premium customer support and supports up to 5,000 trades. Unlimited transactions are supported for $299 per tax season for $199. If you wanted to try it out for free with limited features, you could do that. If you're in the market for a crypto tax software tool, I'd highly recommend it.

But what are the advantages and disadvantages of CryptoTrader.Tax? If you're looking for a tech solution with an intuitive interface, is simple to use, and offers a free trial, this crypto tax tool should definitely be on your shortlist. Given their focus on the US market, I'd also recommend this option if you're based there. In terms of drawbacks, I'd like to see more exchanges support it, and you should be aware that the platform is heavily focused on US and IRS forms. That means that people living in other parts of the world have better options. Finally, who is CryptoTrader.Tax for? In my opinion, this tax solution is ideal for anyone filing crypto taxes in the US, but there is limited leverage trading platform support. So, if that's your thing, you'll probably have to look into other options. All things considered, it's a fairly simple and beginner-friendly game. If you're new to crypto tax calculations, this is an excellent place to begin.

Bear Tax

This tax software solution, similar to CryptoTrader, allows users to compute and file tax reports quickly and easily. Tax was created with the US market in mind, but it can also be used in other countries. Bear.tax was designed with average consumers and financial advisors in mind, so sharing those reports with your accountant will be a breeze. How does it function? Bear.tax, like its competitors, takes a similar approach. This entails either using an API integration or uploading a CSV file with your tradesHowever, you can choose whether to process your report using FIFO or LIFO rules. Finally, Bear, the software will generate the necessary tax documents for your income classification. Tax has a few more options than CryptoTrader. Gifts, staking rewards, airdrops, hard forks, referrals, mining voting rewards, community rewards, inheritances, crypto payments, and earning programs are all supported by the tax. So, if you're using an income source that CryptoTrader doesn't support, you're out of luck. Tax then, you'll probably want to look at Bear. Tax instead.

Another plus is that the platform's unique matching algorithm ensures that transactions are recorded and processed without regard for fees or block time delays. This ensures that you comply with IRS guidelines by recording taxable events while avoiding an over-reporting tax. Quite effective. Bear, for those who HODL-d and didn't consider all of this tax when they started. With a transaction function, the tax has you covered. This allows you to search for and modify specific transactions. As a result, you can be certain that you've entered the correct cost basis for a given time or date. If you initially refused to pay for a cryptocurrency tax software tool, you'll understand the agony of scrolling through Coinmarketcap graphs to look up a coin's previous price. With Bear, that is no longer an issue. For each supported cryptocurrency, the tax provides historical pricing data.

It's also worth noting that this software tool supports BOTS and high-frequency traders. If you've used a BOT like three commas to help automate your trading, Bear.Tax is one of the tax tools you should investigate.

CoinTracking Software

It's jam-packed with cutting-edge tax reporting software to make filing your taxes a breeze. On CoinTracking, you can find a wealth of information, including personal portfolio analysis, trade imports, tax declarations, coin charts, and coin trends. CoinTracking is a popular application. It has over 600,000 active users, as well as over 750 CPAs and corporate clients. This tax software solution is in charge of generating tax reports for 4.3 billion dollars in portfolio holdings. If you're a crypto veteran, CoinTracking has 11 years of historical price data for you. Also, because CoinTracking supports over 7500 coins, any altcoin dumpster divers will be covered. CoinTracking is unique in that it can be used by both crypto traders and businesses. If you're a budding crypto entrepreneur, you should definitely look into this option. This is how it goes. After you import your trades, CoinTracking crunches the numbers for you and returns a wealth of information, including real-time profits, losses, coin value, gain, taxes owed, and more. A series of interactive charts for trades and coins, as well as profit and loss audit reports and an overview for realized and unrealized gains, are included in the personal portfolio analysis feature.

Another cool feature is the ability to import wallet data from Ledger and Trezor, as well as support for a variety of legacy exchanges. MTGox included. You can connect two exchanges using API integration to import those crypto transactions, just like every other crypto tax software tool on this list. Direct blockchain network sync is, however, also possible. Unlike Bear, however. CryptoTrader and Taxes Tax, CoinTracking has a slew of additional tax-computing options. There are twelve of them. This includes the traditional FIFO and LIFO methods, as well as the average cost method and many others. All of this means that CoinTracking is more tax jurisdictions compatible than any of the other solutions I mentioned.

If you've ever done your taxes before, you're well aware of the difficulties that arise when transactions are missing or duplicated. Things aren't balanced, so you'll have to go over each transaction again, which takes time. With coin tracking, that should be a thing of the past, as the software has several methods for verifying transactions that are designed to find missing or duplicate transactions. It has a decent free option for cost coin tracking that supports up to 200 transactions, limited tax and capital gains reporting, coin tracking, and CSV imports. It would be beneficial if you tried before purchasing this tax software to ensure that you are satisfied with it.

The following is important information about paid plans. They are billed on a monthly basis rather than per tax season. For ten dollars a month, the pro plan supports three and a half thousand transactions, prioritized transactions, and customer support. You get everything in the pro plan plus support for up to 20,000 transactions when you upgrade to the expert plan. For $50 per month, you get unlimited transaction support and priority customer service. Now I'd like to discuss the advantages of CoinTracking. It calculates crypto tax using 12 different computation methods, indicating that it is designed to serve a wider range of countries directly. If you live outside of the United States, you should take a look at this.

This solution is ideal for both professional altcoiners and leverage traders because it supports a wide range of coins and exchanges. In terms of disadvantages, the paid plans may be quite costly. If you've only made a few trades this year, I'd suggest going with a less expensive option like Bear. Tax. Who is CoinTracking for, exactly? It's one of my top recommendations for anyone living outside of the United States who has a lot of transactions during the tax year. This is the tax solution you should consider if you are a leveraged trader using buy bit or a low-cap altcoin.

Chapter 30. Companies Enabling Bitcoin Adoption

In the first category of companies, we'll look at our established entities with profitable businesses or businesses on stable ground. Adding BTC to their stable offerings only strengthens them, and as the price of Bitcoin rises, you can expect these companies to gain ground as well.

PayPal

It's the go-to service for merchants and online workers who wish to get paid. While it doesn't have a monopoly, it does have a powerful economic moat that ensures its business will survive tough times.

In October 2020, PayPal announced it would allow cryptocurrency transactions on its platform and process crypto payments to merchants. Currently, the company has 325 million users and 26 million merchants. PayPal has been enabling other ways of withdrawing cryptocurrency before this announcement. It has a good relationship with Coinbase that stretches back to 2016 and has allowed Coinbase users to transfer their fiat money to PayPal since 2018.

PayPal also owns Venmo, and cryptocurrency transactions will be enabled on the latter in 2021. Venmo has recently enabled payments to merchants, increasing the frequency of cryptocurrency transactions on the platform. Investing in PayPal is much more than just about Bitcoin. However, as Bitcoin stands to be adopted by the masses, there's no doubt PayPal will benefit from it and will also enable greater adoption at the same time.

Coinbase

We must point out that Coinbase isn't a public company yet and that retail investors cannot purchase shares in it. However, Coinbase has recently submitted a Form S-1, a strong signal of their intent to file an IPO. As of their last funding round, Coinbase had a valuation of eight billion dollars. This was in 2018. Since then, the demand for its services has increased and along with the value of BTC. As the most significant enabler of cryptocurrency trading in the world, there's no doubt that Coinbase stands to gain from the surge of interest that retail investors have in cryptos. Our conservative estimate places Coinbase's valuation at least double its past valuation. With crypto interest-only continuing to grow, there's no doubt that Coinbase will be a massive IPO play once it debuts on the markets.

Bitmain

Bitmain was founded in 2013, back before BTC or cryptocurrency was considered mainstream as it is today. The company's mission was quite simple. They built (and continue to build) machines that help people mine Bitcoin and cryptocurrencies. Bitmain is headquartered in Beijing, China, and was valued at over $1 billion in 2017, its last funding round. By 2018, the company became the world's largest manufacturer of ASIC chips used to mine BTC. The company also opened other lines of business by running two of the largest BTC mining pools in the world, namely BTC and Antpool. However, note that Bitmain has had its share of controversies, having already been embroiled in high-profile court cases. It was alleged that the company was mining coins on its devices using customer electricity.

Regardless, the company is already profitable and is projected to continue showing profitability going forward. It first planned an IPO in 2018 to be listed on the Hong Kong stock exchange. However, a crash in Bitcoin prices deterred the board from going ahead with its plans. The company is set to proceed with an IPO in mid-2021 in Hong Kong.

This means Robinhood traders won't be able to purchase any stock, but more sophisticated brokerage platforms will give you access to it. The company is expected to raise over $18 billion in its IPO and will become the largest pure-play on cryptocurrency in the markets. Regarding the various "crypto mining" companies listed on the stock market, we are most bullish on Bitmain, and you should be too.

Canaan Inc.

Canaan happens to be the very first company we recommended to our readers back in March 2020. Like Bitmain, this small-cap Chinese company manufactures mining equipment for its customers. Unlike Bitmain, it doesn't have the same degree of backing and has struggled a bit during its tenure. Between June 2019 and June 2020, Canaan's revenues fell by 47%, and the company posted a net loss of $12.3 million by Q3 2020. Its PS ratio is currently 101, which can make it seem like an absurd investment. However, Canaan's fortunes are directly tied to Bitcoin's price. The company was projected to be profitable only if BTC was above $15,000. Currently, BTC is trading at twice that number. Despite this, Canaan is a speculative play and is a risky investment. However, given the boost we expect all crypto mining manufacturers to receive, this company seems set to cash in on the overall sector interest.

Companies that Pivoted

The boom in Bitcoin has led to some extraordinary stories and investment opportunities. The companies we are going to feature next can either be viewed as incompetent or as visionaries. Regardless of the broader perception, we believe they stand to gain immensely from the surge of interest in BTC and cryptocurrency because they have decided to tie their fortunes directly to it.

Riot Blockchain

We have to discuss Riot Blockchain by mentioning that this company's stock surged by 1,500% in 2020 with increased BTC's price. And that's not all; the company's story itself is pretty strange. Back in 2017, this company was a biotech startup with just six employees. At some point, the founders saw the writing on the wall and decided to pivot to mining cryptocurrencies.

In December 2019, the company bought 15,000 Antminer S19 Bitcoin mining rigs from Bitmain back in 2019 when the cost of mining cryptocurrency was higher than the value of the coins themselves. This marked a capacity increase of 33% for them. The company kept mining coins and is now profiting from a surge in the value of BTC. However, dealing with energy costs is still a challenge for them. Practically, no one on Wall Street knows what to make of this company. However, if you are on the lookout for a company that hoards a large amount of BTC, Riot Blockchain is it.

MicroStrategy

MicroStrategy is probably not an accurate description of what this company does as far as company names go. There's nothing micro about it, and the management doesn't seem to have much of a strategy either. This company produces business intelligence software and cloud-based services for its clients. It was founded in 1989 when its founder landed a consulting contract with DuPont and $250,000 as seed capital. MicroStrategy went from strength to strength as it brought a rigid analytical framework to its clients' sales data and enabled them to make better business decisions. At one point in the mid-90s, the company included McDonald's in one of its many clients.

The 90s was a successful decade for them, and they decided to go public at the turn of the millennium. The company began to go pear-shaped soon after. It kept releasing products that were well received by the market, but the lack of quality started drawing attention. The company started erroneously exaggerating its accounting results as more clients left the company. A SEC fine followed, and layoffs began. A decade later, it didn't seem like MicroStrategy had much of a future. As the last Hail Mary, the company pivoted to creating business intelligence tools and providing cloud software analytics platforms for its clients, hoping to gain from the boom in big data. This hasn't panned out very well either since the company lacks the technical know-how to compete with other intelligence tools providers like Sisense or IBM.

Are you wondering why we have included this company on this list? Well, it happens to hold an insane amount of BTC. In August 2020, the company announced it was moving $250 million of reserve cash into BTC. This amount increased over the following months, and as of December 1, 2020, the company held 70,470 BTC, valued at over $1 billion. By the end of January 2021, they had reached $2.2 Billion. Microstrategy's BTC position now dwarfs the rest of their business by a significant amount.

This interest in BTC, combined with an increase in its price, saw Microstrategy's stock price surge by almost 400% in the past 12 months, roughly in line with the increase in BTC prices. However, there is some confusion regarding the company's strategy because, unlike Riot Blockchain, MicroStrategy is not a miner. The company simply bought BTC with its cash on hand. They even borrowed money to buy coins, and they do not plan on using them in any way to augment the current business. The company also does not have any plans to pivot to the cryptocurrency sector. This is probably a good thing, though, given the company's track record. By all accounts,

MicroStrategy was a company going nowhere. However, today it happens to be sitting on a goldmine. Its price is divorced from its core business, and if you want a speculative play on the price of BTC without actually buying any coins, MicroStrategy is a good bet.

The Best Blockchain ETFs

Whenever a growth industry like blockchain emerges, several investment banks and market makers will launch their own ETFs to capitalize on the interest in the sector. Blockchain is no different, and in the past 12 months alone, some new ETFs have been launched.

Many of these are thinly traded and thus are subject to manipulation. Therefore, when buying an ETF, the two most important metrics are volume and assets under management. With both of these metrics, the larger the better strategy always works.

The most well-rounded blockchain ETF is the Siren Nasdaq NexGen Economic ETF, which trades under the ticker symbol BLCN. Compared to its competitors, it has a lower expense ratio (0.68%) and a well-diversified holding of 70 companies. Owning BLCN gives you exposure to crypto mining manufacturers like Canaan Inc (the second-largest holding), as well as financial companies set to benefit from the BTC boom like Square and Signature Bank. There are other blockchains ETFs on the market like KOIN and BLOK, but BLCN remains our preferred one.

Chapter 31. Common Myths, Mistakes, & Misconceptions about Bitcoin

If you've been reading along, you should feel pretty confident that, at this point, you have a handle on the basics of Bitcoin and blockchain technology. You have the tools in your toolkit to set up a Bitcoin wallet, get yourself some Bitcoin, and make transactions. That being said, to hit the ground running, there are a few common misconceptions about Bitcoin that are worth covering to avoid falling into traps, making mistakes, or getting tricked.

Anonymity: Is Bitcoin Anonymous?

Something that is often mentioned in the news about Bitcoin is that it is "anonymous." This has created much confusion, but the short answer is: *No, Bitcoin is not anonymous!*

We know that Bitcoin transactions are recorded on the blockchain as transfers from one public Bitcoin address. There are ways to increase the level of privacy surrounding transactions, but anonymity is not necessarily achieved by default when looked at in context.

For example, when you buy Bitcoin with fiat currency from an exchange linked to your bank account, such as Coinbase, your funds are deposited into a particular Bitcoin wallet address. In this scenario, there is a clear link between your bank account to your Bitcoin address.

Because every Bitcoin transaction is stored, forever, on the publicly accessible blockchain, anyone can observe the activity of a particular wallet's public address. In theory, it is possible to achieve anonymity by avoiding any behavior that might link a wallet's public address to that wallet's owner. In practice, however, when converting between Bitcoin and fiat, information about a user's identity often becomes public or at least accessible to third parties. It is best to proceed with the assumption that Bitcoin is secure but not anonymous by default.

Is Bitcoin Taxable?

Often under the past misconception that Bitcoin is "anonymous" or "untraceable," many people assume that Bitcoin is not subject to taxes. This is wrong, at least in most countries.

In the US, the IRS treats Bitcoin and other forms of digital currency as an asset, like property, not as a currency. This means that you will be subject to capital gain or loss when dealing with digital currency. Additionally, if you are getting paid in Bitcoin, your income is also tax either as an individual or a business. According to the IRS, taxpayers must report transactions made in Bitcoin according to their value in US dollars.

An in-depth analysis of tax law about Bitcoin is beyond the scope of this book. Still, for serious Bitcoin investors, it is essential to do your homework to avoid getting into trouble with the IRS.

Do Criminals Use Bitcoin

While popular media such as TV shows and movies have certainly played a role in introducing Bitcoin into the mainstream, it is almost always portrayed as being used for illicit transactions in some criminal context. It has even been suggested that Bitcoin is used primarily by terrorists! While it is true that illegal goods and services are sold online, particularly on the "darknet," the reality is that the vast majority of Bitcoin users are not involved in criminal activity.

In large part due to the public ledger of transactions, and, once again, the fact that Bitcoin is not anonymous by default, Bitcoin is not an ideal currency for conducting illegal transactions. To this point, the famous Winkelvoss Twins, founders of the popular Gemini Bitcoin exchange, have suggested that Bitcoin is only used by "stupid criminals."

The conflating of Bitcoin with shady dealings is due in no small part to the incident mentioned above with the popular Mt. Gox exchange. The dubious circumstances surrounding the loss of a vast number of Bitcoins from Mt. Gox led to many reports that painted Bitcoin itself as the culprit rather than the poor management of the Mt. Gox exchange. Similarly, when the famous "Silk Road" website, used mainly for selling illegal drugs and other items through the dark web, was shut down by the FBI in 2013, many people conflated this incident with Bitcoin itself being "shut down."

Bitcoin can be difficult to understand. It is easy to see how much media coverage in the earlier days of Bitcoin failed to distinguish between Bitcoin itself and various platforms built on top of it, such as Silk Road and Mt. Gox. Today, public opinion is changing rapidly as Bitcoin is gaining traction all over the world. However, there are still many people out there who are under the impression that there is something inherently illicit or illegal about Bitcoin.

Is Bitcoin a Ponzi Scheme?

"Ponzi Scheme" has become a buzzword about many cryptocurrencies. There are some "alt-coins" out there that might be Ponzi Schemes, but Bitcoin is not one of them.

Ponzi Schemes work by promising huge rewards to entice investors to put money into a never really actualized concept. Bitcoin's decentralized structure means no CEO or "head of Bitcoin" to defraud investors. Furthermore, Bitcoin has never made any guarantees concerning market value. Anybody familiar with Bitcoin will tell you that it is incredibly volatile, and there is no knowing if it will go up or down on any given day. Finally, the defining characteristic of a Ponzi Scheme is that it offers no real value. We see new examples of real-world applications of Bitcoin and blockchain technology across various industries on an almost daily basis, backed by a broad consensus within the tech community that this is a revolutionary technology that will not go away any time soon.

Bitcoin Uses Too Much Energy and Is Bad for the Environment

Bitcoin miners do use a lot of electricity. Clickbait news like to compare bitcoin miners' electricity usage to that of small countries. Of course, the same critique might be made of the Internet, which uses 10% of global electricity. You will have to decide whether cat videos and clickbait news about bitcoin's energy usage are a good use of global electricity. I think that the Internet is worth it. Higher civilizations use more energy than low civilizations. If you live in a mud hut, your energy consumption will be deficient. If you are part of a globally connected space-faring civilization, your energy usage will be much, much higher. Fortunately, there are nearly infinite energy sources in the solar system. Fusion and Dyson spheres will power our global civilization to the next level.

It's also unfair to criticize bitcoin's energy usage without examining the trade-offs. Mining gold uses vast amounts of energy and can be quite hard on the environment. The fiat financial system also uses a lot of energy. Think of all those Brinks trucks and ATMs and perpetually empty bank branches with their heating and lighting costs. Printing up new paper money and coins also uses large amounts of natural resources and energy. Then there is the financial cost of human energy that is confiscated through monetary inflation.

No one criticizes a bank or brokerage (or Fort Knox) for using a lot of energy to secure wealth. You can't just leave gold bars out in the open—they require physical security. Bank and brokerage accounts also require digital or cryptographic security, both of which use electricity.

Bitcoin is the most secure bank in the cloud. It's secured by real work carried out by bitcoin mining computers. The high hash rate of the bitcoin network (and associated high energy costs) ensures that it's a safe and secure place to store wealth. Bitcoin is a scarce, decentralized, seizure-resistant, and censorship-resistant way to store value. Why should something like that be free or low cost? Would you ever consider using a low-cost solution to secure a Picasso painting or the Hope Diamond?

Many people don't realize that a substantial amount of bitcoin mining is powered by renewable energy (solar, wind, hydropower) or "stranded" energy sources. Stranded natural gas is often flared or vented into the atmosphere if it's not cost-efficient to build a pipeline to move the gas. Companies are now using this stranded natural gas to power bitcoin mining machines rather than being wasted like this.

Bitcoin Is a Bubble

There has never been a bubble that popped and then came back to new highs just a few years later. People who don't have a lot of experience with markets will often call a particular market a bubble. Observers have been calling the California housing market a bubble for the past 50 years, and yet housing prices continue to march higher almost every year. Amazon was called a bubble but turned out to be simply one of the best businesses of all time. Just because an asset like

Apple or Amazon goes up a lot in price doesn't mean that it's a bubble.

Now that bitcoin is hitting new all-time highs once again, the burden of proof is on the critics. What would they need to see for their hypothesis to be falsified? Peter Schiff has been declaring that bitcoin is a bubble since 2013 when trading at $375. Why would anyone continue to listen to him?

Bitcoin Has No Value Because Anyone Can Easily Create Their Cryptocurrency

Anyone can fork (copy) the bitcoin software, but no one can fork the bitcoin ecosystem. You can create your cryptocurrency, but how will you persuade all of the total nodes, miners, developers, and investors to accept your new cryptocurrency? I can easily create my social networking software, but it doesn't mean that I will steal users from Facebook. The real value is in the network of people who interact with the software rather than the software itself.

A Competitor Will Replace Bitcoin

Bitcoin is a money protocol. The Internet still runs on old protocols like TCP/IP, HTTP, and SMTP. In a perfect world, they would be better, but they stick around because they are "good enough." Bitcoin does an excellent job of securing value in a trustless, uncensorable manner. Bitcoin is "good enough." Facebook supplanted MySpace because it didn't cost anything to open up an account on both networks. It's impossible to store your savings simultaneously in bitcoin and a new competing cryptocurrency without first selling off some of your bitcoin and using it to purchase the new crypto.

Its strong network effects protect Bitcoin. Buyers go to Amazon because all of the sellers are there; sellers go to Amazon because that is where all of the buyers are. Bitcoin has the largest market cap, highest security (highest hash rate), and highest liquidity of any cryptocurrency, making it an ideal candidate for institutional investors. This creates a virtuous circle where bitcoin gets even more prominent and more secure the more institutional investors to buy it.

Bitcoin is good at doing some fundamental things—storing value and making it possible to send that value anywhere in the world. If you added more bells and whistles, it would only increase the attack surface of bitcoin. Over time, additional layers will be built on bitcoin (like the Lightning Network, for example). But the foundation will stay the same. Only bitcoin can offer this highly secure, neutral, global settlement layer.

Chapter 32. Top 10 Crypto Investing Websites

Investing in bitcoins is rage, but how do you get started?

Do you need bitcoins to invest? Or do you transfer money from your bank account somewhere and transfer it to bitcoin? What is it?

In the future, we will use BTC, which is a symbol of bitcoin on exchanges and trading platforms. If you just want to make a high profit with cryptocurrencies, you can consider a cryptocurrency savings account. These accounts pay up to 12% but have a risk (like regular cryptocurrencies).

How to Invest in Bitcoin

Investing in BTC is similar to investing in stocks, except that volatility is much more substantial due to BTC's daily volatility. These are stocks investment steps from the beginning:

- Open a brokerage account with a company that allows cryptocurrencies
- Deposit money from your bank to the broker's account.
- Buy shares with a deposit (cash balance).
- Then sell the stock to make a profit or lose. The money is returned to your cash balance.

The main difference from BTC is the third step; you buy BTC or another cryptocurrency instead of stocks.

With BTC, the above flow is similar in most cases, but it depends on the exchange. In some cases, you can purchase BTC by credit card or by transferring money from your bank account. For other platforms, you must transfer BTC directly. These are called BTC direct deposits.

We will discuss how to invest in BTC for US citizens. The methods differ from country to country due to differences in legislation and regulations. Some countries require more private information than others to prove their legitimacy.

How to Deposit US Dollars to Buy Bitcoins and Cryptocurrencies

Coinbase is one of the most popular platforms and has a simple process. Some of the websites mentioned below will follow a similar process. We love Coinbase because you get $5 for opening an account. Coinbase account can be open with Coinbase and connect to your bank account or credit card. Then transfer money from your bank account to purchase BTC or purchase by credit card. Buying a BTC with a credit card is the most expensive.

The mechanism for buying BTC involves entering either the amount of US dollars or the amount of BTC. The website then converts to another currency. For example, if you enter $500, the website will fill in BTC 0.0357 (or what the current BTC exchange rate is).

After filling in the total amount, click to purchase your BTC. Although credit card transactions are the most expensive, they are also the fastest way to complete a BTC transaction.

A bank account can take up to several days. Remember that you will receive an exchange rate when you buy BTC. If the BTC increases by 1000 by the time your transaction is completed in three days, you will miss the increase. Where exactly did you buy BTC? After all, you haven't invested in yet. Your BTC is in a so-called digital wallet. Almost all exchanges have their wallet, which you use to store BTC.

Going back to the broker's example, your cash balance is used for trading stocks. The BTC in your wallet is used for trading BTC.

How about Your US Dollars?

There is room in your wallet for BTC and USD. If you deposited $10,000 and bought $5,000 BTC, your wallet would look like this:

$ 5,000

0.34 BTC

A wallet is a big topic of discussion when it comes to cryptocurrencies. We won't detail them, but you can use a standalone wallet if you don't want to use an exchange wallet. Electrum.org is an example of a standalone example. These can be desktop, mobile, or websites.

You can even use a hardware wallet such as LedgerWallet. Once you have made a deposit on the options exchange and purchased BTC, you are ready to invest. Trading platforms on exchanges are very similar to brokerage platforms. You will have a chart and buy/sell buttons with the BTC amount to trade. By trading BTC, you can exchange it for other cryptocurrencies, which is another way to sell BTC. Or you can exchange it from another cryptocurrency for BTC, like buying BTC.

Send BTC Directly

If the exchange does not allow you to purchase BTC by money transfer or credit card, you can deposit BTC from another exchange. This is done by getting the address of your wallet from the target exchange. Then import it to the original exchange together with the BTC amount to transfer to the new exchange. Transactions take a few minutes for the exchanged BTC to appear in the target wallet.

Here is our list of the ten most popular bitcoins and cryptocurrencies.

1. Coinbase

coinbase

Open An Account

Get $5 free!

As we mentioned above, Coinbase is the most popular today because you can invest directly in US dollars. Currently, you can buy bitcoin, Etherum, and Litecoin, and more than 30 other coins and tokens on the platform. Also, you can earn interest on your USDT and receive rewards for symbols by performing various actions.

Besides, by opening a Coinbase account, you will receive $5 bonuses!

2. Gemini

GEMINI

Open An Account

Gemini is a popular platform for investing in cryptocurrencies due to its focus on security and transparency. Unlike some exchanges that seem vulnerable, Gemini makes it central to protecting its customers. When you open an account in Gemini and deposit $100, you will receive ten bonus dollars!

3. BlockFi

Open An Account

BlockFi is a cryptocurrency investment platform that allows you to borrow and earn interest on your holdings. Besides, instead of selling your coins and tokens, you can also borrow the money you own. If you just want to keep your tokens, you can also let them earn interest for you.

Bonus Offer: Receive a bonus of up to $250 when you make a deposit of $25 and keep it for the specified period.

4. Kraken

Open An Account

Kraken was one of the original platforms for cryptocurrency trading, and they have a good selection of coins and tokens for trading and investing. They also allow you to trade on margins. However, this is an actual exchange and not as easy to use as some of the best platforms on this list.

Kraken is one of the few platforms on this list that allows you to trade with DOGE and other, riskier tokens.

5. Robinhood

Robinhood

Open An Account

Get a free share of stock!

Robinhood allows free crypto trades on their platform. They are available in just a few states and using only Bitcoin and Ethereum, but there are plans on expanding this quickly. There are limitations, but it's free! Also, when you open a Robinhood account, you get a free share of stock!

6. eToro

eToro

Open An Account

eToro has been around for some time in the UK and across Europe, but they now allow retailers in the US. They offer a wide selection of digital assets to buy and sell on their platform, and even better—they have a real trading account, so you can try it before you use real money.

eToro now offers a $50 bonus for new customers who open accounts and trade $1,000 in cryptocurrency until May 15, 2021. This advertisement encourages virtual cryptocurrencies in the European Union (eToro Europe Ltd. and eToro UK Ltd.) and the United States (eToro USA LLC); which is very volatile, is not controlled in most EU countries, has no protection from the EU, and is not controlled by the EU legal framework. Investments are filled with market risk, so also loss of principal.

7. Bitcoin IRA

BITCOINIRA

Open An Account

The Bitcoin IRA is somewhat different from other platforms here. Unlike most exchanges and wallets, you just exchange currencies and pay taxes on your earned money (here's how taxation of your cryptocurrencies works.). With this in mind, the bitcoin IRA best combines a cryptocurrency wallet and an exchange, as well as an IRA. This means that your account income is not taxed or deferred.

8. Crypto

crypto.com

Open An Account

Crypto is one of the largest and fastest-growing cryptocurrency exchanges. Headquartered in Hong Kong, it offers significant support to consumers in the

United States. You can now access more than 90 tokens and coins worldwide and 50 tokens and coins if you are in the United States. Also, this offer provides a stable rate for their crypto-savings accounts.

The only major drawback is that it is currently based on a program rather than a desktop.

9. Binance

A great platform to participate in multiple currencies such as Cardano or Neo. Not as easy to use as some of the best platforms on this list. They have an excellent mobile application, but again, not easy to use.

Open An Account

Note: Binance.us is the US version of the platform and has a limited amount and tokens to invest compared to the international version of Binance.

10. Hodlnaut

Open An Account

Hodlnaut makes a difference by becoming a platform for cryptocurrencies that allows you to earn significant interest in your crypto holdings. It doesn't support as many tokens as the others on this list, but it pays some of the highest rates compared to other platforms here. Also, they offer digital asset loans on their platform.

Stocks investment and that of BTC are not much different. With BTC, you need to open an account on the stock exchange. With shares, you open an account in a brokerage company. Then you deposit money. The only difference when investing in BTC is that you have to buy BTC first using a markup before trading BTC. However, your first purchase of BTC is your first discovery.

Chapter 33. Terminologies Used in the Cryptocurrency World

Some are pretty common, while others are less mentioned.

51% Attack describes the monopoly of a single individual or group of the entity on a particular network's computing power. As the single individual or entity owns a more significant percentage, they dominate the web. Should they choose to, they can affect cryptocurrency destructively. The destruction may occur via several means such as reusing coins, halting mining, putting a stop to, or even changing transactions.

Addresses are often a combination of over 30 characters and unique in appearance to each cryptocurrency. All cryptocurrency coins have embedded within them and address specific to them that highlights their position on the blockchain. The address stores all the pertinent information concerning the owners and records any changes made during trading.

Airdrop – airdrops are bonuses awarded to a few people who can be members of the present assembly or low-ranked brokers. The cryptocurrency owner freely gives these coins as gifts or returns for tasks such as creating awareness among colleagues and acquaintances. Airdrops are a great marketing strategy that allows for distribution and acknowledgment among the community.

Algorithm – Algorithms are a series of instructions mathematically imputed and executed by computer software. It is ideally intended to guarantee the achievement of the wanted results.

All-Time High – It's the extreme amount reached by said cryptocurrency.

All-Time Low – The lowermost amount attained by said cryptocurrency.

Altcoins – This is the original cryptocurrency, bitcoin is prosperous, and it's pretty popular. The other cryptocurrencies which sprang up subsequently after bitcoin are collectively labeled Altcoins. They include Ethereum, Ripple, LiteCoins, among others.

AML – The abbreviation of the phrase "Anti-Money Laundering."

Anti-Money Laundering – These are the international laws and guidelines set up to ensure that criminal elements, similar to the mafia or syndicates, do not exploit cryptocurrencies to launder cash.

Application Specific Integrated Circuit – A piece of hardware built just like any other, the application-specific integrated circuit is designed for the significant purpose of mining cryptocurrency. With this hardware, the major mining problem, the hashing problems, are solved.

Arbitrage – Cryptocurrency is acquired and traded at varying fees at once and at the exact location. When the purchase and sale of said cryptocurrency bring about a net profit, then arbitrage has occurred.

ASIC – An abbreviation of the phrase "Application Specific Integrated Circuit."

ATH – An abbreviation of the phrase "All-Time High."

ATL – An abbreviation of the phrase "All Time Low."

Atomic Swap – Atomic swap provides a lucrative and swift way of changing one form of cryptocurrency to another, devoid of the need to acquire and peddle cryptocurrency.

Bag – It's the accumulation of a substantial quantity of cryptocurrency.

Bear/Bearish – The descending dive in the value of cryptocurrency.

Bear Trap – As suggested, the bear trap is a ruse carried out by a few dealers to trap the market. These people conspire and sell their cryptocurrencies at once. This then fools the market into believing they know something that others do not, and a crash is imminent. Other traders react to the sudden sales and quickly sell their assets, further reducing prices. The original brokers who had set the trap recover their investments and buy many others at meager prices, making a tidy profit when the prices rebound.

Bitcoin – Created by Satoshi Nakamoto in 2008, bitcoin was introduced to the world as a regional, equal electronic cash system.

Block – A block is a vault jam-packed with material about all the records concerning cryptocurrency transactions. Several blocks are the framework of a blockchain. The information stored within the block can be retrieved at will by anyone.

Block Explorer – Blockchains can be monitored via a block explorer. An important available device, the block explorer, allows viewers to observe all agreements that happened. They also help evaluate all activities and offer any additional data, for instance, coin stream, total network hash rate, transaction growth, and so forth.

Block Height – The number of blocks in a chain makes up the block height. The block height begins from height 0, which is the genesis lock.

Block Reward – Several miners work hard to decipher the hash or verifications within a block. Those who successfully figure it out are compensated. The compensations are awarded because by verifying the dealings on the blockchain, and more coins come up for grabs. These are awarded to miners for a job well done are referred to as block reward.

Blockchain – The blockchain is a greatly favored choice because it's regional mainly. Millions of computers all around the globe all have access to the same material on the blockchains. There is no principal copy hidden somewhere, and this fact is even more imperative. This is a culmination of separate blocks, all of which contain information about the dealings made about a specific cryptocurrency. All of them make up the chain are bound together by what is known as the cryptographic signature.

BTFD – An abbreviation of the phrase "Buy The F$%king Dip."

Bull/Bullish – The rising projection in the value of a cryptocurrency.

Burned – Cryptocurrency coins that cannot be spent are said to be burned.

Buy the F$%king Dip – It's the rude manner of announcing to everyone that there is a dip in a specific coinage. This phrase is often used to persuade dealers to purchase a currency whose significance has momentarily reduced.

Buy Wall – A buy wall is an order that permits the sale of a cryptocurrency at a stated amount. This is a common enough one as it guarantees that the price of a cryptocurrency does not go below a set value. It is also essential because demand will be far more than supply once the directive is implemented.

CAP – It's a shorthand usage of the phrase "market capitalization."

Central Ledger – A central ledger is a singular entity that contains all the information about the financial archives.

Chain Linking – All forms of cryptocurrency have their blockchain. When there is a swap between two different cryptocurrency types, then two other blockchains are involved. Those two are then linked together in a process called chain linking to ensure a successful transaction.

Cipher – Information can be encrypted and decrypted by a particular algorithm. The said algorithm is called a cipher.

Circulating Supply – Not all cryptocurrency coins are available in circulation. Some are locked for future use, reserved for several reasons, or burned and are unusable. Therefore, the number available for spending is limited, which is acknowledged as the circulating supply.

Cold Storage – An alternative way of saying paper wallets.

Confirmed – Transactions that have been affirmed by the network and affixed to the blockchain are called confirmed transactions.

Consensus – Confirmed dealings on the network and those successfully bound to the blockchain are known as consensus transactions.

Consensus Process – There are several nodes on a network that tests for a business deal's authenticity. These are named the consensus process. They ensure that all authentic dealings are affixed to the blockchain.

Consortium Blockchain – A consortium blockchain is a blockchain that is retained and maintained by an independent party. Despite that, the blockchain is also transparent in a public manner.

Cryptocurrency – Cryptocurrency is a substitute type of currency that is not dependent on any bank. It is an encrypted and arithmetical type of money that is crafted and managed with erudite mathematics.

Cryptographic Hash Function – This only transpires on a node when it endeavors to modify an instruction like a transmission to the blockchain in the form of an established, encoded, numerical string. This alteration is regulated via a hashing procedure. There are many algorithms available for cryptocurrencies.

Cryptography – The practice of coding and decoding information is known as cryptography.

DAO – An abbreviation of the phrase "decentralized autonomous organization."

dApp – It's an abbreviation of the phrase "decentralized application."

Decentralized Application – A computer software program that ensures the blockchains are well used as data storage. It provides the blockchain runs independently, without control from outside forces, open sources, and offers incentives and vouchers.

Decentralized Autonomous Organization – These are administrations that operate independently of individual contribution. This makes sure that no individual or body has total autonomy over the system but that everyone is immersed in the program's running.

Deflation – Deflation arises when the request for a cryptocurrency is significantly reduced.

Depth Chart – The depth chart is the visual representation of the bids, otherwise called the requests to buy against the proposals to sell. The linear picture indicates the theoretical phases when the market can conduct business transactions at different prices at various stages. With the graph, it's easy to see any essential buy walls or sell walls in the equation.

Deterministic Wallet – To make a deterministic wallet, seeds are needed to produce multiple keys. That way, even if it gets lost, the tickets will be recouped from the root. With a wallet, there would be no need to make new keys for every transaction. This makes transfers and storage much more accessible.

Difficulty – In cryptocurrency, this means a rise in the current charge of mining. If several dealings are operating concurrently, this results in the division of the network nodes. This then results in difficulty. More significant problems result in more extensive transaction fees.

Digital Commodity – A challenging, imperceptible resource that holds great value and can only be moved electronically.

Digital Currency – Also known as a numerical commodity.

Digital Signature – This guarantees the authenticity of a transferred document. It often shows as a cipher created via public key encryption.

Distributed Ledger – Cryptocurrency describes distributed ledger as blockchains that anyone could observe and whenever.

Double Spend – Sending cryptocurrencies to desperate wallets at once is termed double-spending.

Dump – Whenever a dealer sells a more significant percentage of all available cryptocurrencies, it's known as a dump.

Dumping – When several dealers decide to dump simultaneously, it often results in a sharp dip in cryptocurrency value.

Dust Transaction – For several reasons, a few might want a slow network. They achieve this by intentionally inundating the web with a few minute deals. The infinitesimal dealings are called dust transactions.

DYOR – It's an abbreviation of the phrase "do your research."

Encryption – Simply the use of a cipher to convert plain text to incomprehensible text.

ERC – An abbreviation of the phrase "Ethereum requests for comments." It stands for all the supposed improvements made to the Ethereum system.

ERC-20 – This a basic standard of the Ethereum token compilation. It outlines the behaviors of every Ethereum token, making them highly predictable. Because it has done its job well, other cryptocurrencies use ERC-20.

Escrow – Funds in escrow are held by an intermediary between the spender and the receiver.

Ethereum – Ethereum is a widespread cryptocurrency among the top three in the world. It is open-sourced and uses blockchain technology. It has two stark differences from bitcoin; it allows its developers to make apps and write small indentures.

Ethereum Virtual Machine – It's a cybernetic mechanism that works with the network nodes during blockchain confirmations. The Ethereum virtual machine, which is in the cloud, gives the node the freedom to make random EVM Byte Code.

EVM – An abbreviation of the phrase "Ethereum Virtual Machine."

Exchange – Cryptocurrencies are swapped with one another and authorized cash on a stage known as an exchange. There are several currency conversions and fee structures in various exchange platforms.

Chapter 34. How Cryptocurrencies Are Changing the Global Economy and Market Perspectives

The Future of Cryptocurrency

2017 was a big year for cryptocurrency. Many cryptocurrencies saw much growth, with some like Bitcoin, Bitcoin Cash, Dash, and Ethereum seeing exponential growth. As we move forward, the crypto space will only keep growing. According to some industry experts, the coming year will see mass public awareness for cryptocurrencies. Here are some of the things expected to happen in the crypto world within the following year.

Taxation Will Become a Huge Issue

In the coming year, you can expect that the IRS will be more focused on clamping down on cryptocurrency investors to make sure they pay their taxes.

Number of Users Will Rise

There is no doubt that the number of cryptocurrency users is going to increase in the next year. Some industry experts predict that more than 50 million people will hold at least one cryptocurrency in the next year.

Bitcoin to Develop into a Payment Network

Though this was meant to be an electronic payment system, many people currently consider Bitcoin a store of value and a speculative asset. However, according to Trevor Koverko, CEO of a cryptocurrency technology company, Bitcoin's utility and price will increase dramatically, leading to its emergence as a fully-fledged payment network. This will be driven by the development of scaling solutions such as the lightning network. However, for Bitcoin to become an entire payment network, the community needs to adopt these upgrades.

Cryptocurrencies Are Here to Stay

To some people, cryptocurrencies are a fad that will lose momentum as fast as they gained. However, industry experts believe that cryptocurrencies and blockchain technology are here to stay. Some platforms like Neo and Ethereum will push the adoption of technology since they help people create blockchain applications that have meaningful uses in the real world. Adopting these real-world applications by the corporate world will increase the demand for cryptocurrencies and ensure their longevity.

Diversification of Assets by Investors

Currently, most investors hold their assets in Bitcoin and Ethereum. However, you can expect more people to diversify their portfolios into other cryptocurrencies like Dash, Litecoin, Iota, NEM, and many more. Many investors will diversify their crypto assets in much the same way that they approach other traditional investments. Many more cryptocurrencies will also come up in the coming year. Some will be introduced to tackle the challenges experienced by existing cryptocurrencies, while others will add new niches altogether. There is a high likelihood that some of the new cryptocurrencies will become very profitable.

Increased Interest from Institutional Investors

Up until recently, institutional investors have been looking at cryptocurrencies with a very skeptical eye. However, the year 2017 saw the entry of some big-name institutions into the industry. According to the crypto company CEO Mike Poutre, the coming year will see decreased volatility in the price of Bitcoin, which will, in turn, attract more institutional investors and lead to the growth of alternative cryptocurrencies. Mike even predicts that the increased interest from institutional investors might push the market cap of the cryptocurrency industry past the $5 trillion marks in the next year.

Increased Regulation

Currently, many countries do not have any policies regarding cryptocurrencies. However, several governments have been keenly watching their usage and growth. As more people adopt cryptocurrencies, governments will start putting in place regulations surrounding their use. Some financial institutions like Barclays Bank are also trying to push for adopting cryptocurrencies and blockchain technology into the conventional financial system. ICOs are most likely to be the first area to be affected by regulation before they move on to cryptocurrencies themselves. Most rules might also seek to promote the adoption of KYC (know your customer) laws to track the flow of funds and improve transparency. While it is impossible to predict the impact of regulation on cryptocurrencies, there is a high likelihood that such restrictions will not hinder their growth.

Cryptocurrencies Will Force Conventional Financial Systems to Level Up

Currently, banks and traditional payment processors are enjoying extremely high transaction fees. They are also very slow, with most international transactions being processed in 1-3 days. Cryptocurrencies, on the other hand, are swift and have meager processing fees. These advantages might push more businesses to cryptocurrencies. If they are to remain relevant, banks and traditional payment processors will need to up their game.

Despite still being in its infancy stage, cryptocurrency is silently and steadily revolutionizing the world, particularly the financial and investment sector. Due to the many advantages of cryptocurrency, many businesses and individuals are gradually starting to accept this. Many investors have also switched from traditional investment assets to crypto assets. In the last two years, the industry has also created many overnight millionaires and billionaires. Since the industry is still in the initial stages, we can expect that there will be some challenges and hurdles to be overcome before it achieves mainstream adoption. However, we can be confident that the cryptocurrency industry will be the next revolution in the world as we know it.

Conclusion

In conclusion, Bitcoin and cryptocurrency trading for beginners is not easy. However, once you understand the mechanics of it all, many more people will notice the currency. For currency traders, this is an excellent opportunity to make money while so many others struggle with currency swings and inflation. To make money, there needs to be some understanding of risk management, too, though. Finally, I would say that Bitcoin offers an exciting opportunity for all players to make money with trading.

You're not going to earn a living trading cryptocurrency, but you may have the opportunity to make some money trading it. Here are the main points about cryptocurrency trading for beginners:

- Mining is a time-consuming and expensive endeavor.
- Setting up an account on an exchange (or two) may prove economical in terms of capital requirements.
- The cost of mining equipment can vary from purchase to purchase, and equipment's electricity usage is contingent on certain things such as network difficulty as well as the cost of electricity in your country.
- Cryptocurrency exchanges trade currency pairs that are based on the value of one cryptocurrency against another.
- Trading cryptocurrencies can be profitable, but it is not easy to become an expert in technology so that you can trade with confidence.

- Tax laws are different from country to country and may change as regulations and laws around trading change.

- Bitcoin ATMs are also available in some cities worldwide, where you can exchange cash for Bitcoin (and vice versa), though not all ATMs provide such transactions because they are set up by owners machines who decide what kinds of transactions they will allow for.

- Learning about how to trade Bitcoin and other cryptocurrencies may be pretty helpful, and it is possible that you could have the opportunity to earn more by trading than you would through mining.

- The amount you pay for electricity will affect your profits or losses on the equipment you use for mining.

- Cryptocurrency trading has been devaluing miners' returns throughout 2017. Still, it is essential to note that this trend is not guaranteed to continue at the current devaluation rate.

- New cryptocurrency forks are being created all of the time (Bitcoin Cash is one example), resulting in free money when they are worth something.

- However, there is no guarantee that these forks will see the continued value, and they could be worthless in the future.

- According to experts, Bitcoin has reached its peak value.

- After this point, it may go down in value: "There is a lot of debate surrounding the best way to invest your money in an asset. Some believe bitcoin is a solid investment, while others believe that there are better choices out there for you. One thing is certain; if you were buying stocks when Bitcoin was at its absolute highest, you would have seen your investments drop dramatically in the last year."

- Some confidence needs to be placed into the ability of cryptocurrencies and those who use them to survive.
- It is recommended that you may want to invest in other cryptocurrencies as well, as it would be hard to know whether Bitcoin will continue to be the one that dominates the market or not.
- It is also recommended that you look at the different types of cryptocurrencies available, which can help you determine whether a blockchain-based project is worth investing in or not.
- The long-term potential for cryptocurrency trading is still unknown, and many predictions about its future are hard to make.
- For instance, some experts have stated that the market could experience a bubble and burst within the next three months.
- The volatility of Bitcoin itself is pretty high, making it difficult to predict the currency's price very quickly.

www.ingramcontent.com/pod-product-compliance
Lightning Source LLC
LaVergne TN
LVHW022038200926
848481LV00003B/718